EBOOKS

and the

SCHOOL LIBRARY PROGRAM

A Practical Guide for the School Librarian

CATHY LEVERKUS   SHANNON ACEDO

ISBN: 978-0-8389-8672-1

Published by:
American Association of School Librarians
a division of the American Library Association
50 E. Huron St.
Chicago, Illinois 60611-2795

To order, call 800-545-2433, press 7
<www.alastore.ala.org/aasl>

 ACKNOWLEDGMENTS

AASL gratefully acknowledges the following:

Written by:
Cathy Leverkus
Director of Library and Media Services
The Willows Community School (DK-8)
Culver City, California
<cathyl@thewillows.org>

Shannon Acedo
Chair, Library and Information Technology Department
Harvard-Westlake Upper School
Studio City, California
<sacedo@hw.com>

AASL Staff Liaison: Stephanie Book

TABLE OF CONTENTS

 INTRODUCTION

Why focus on the school library ebook collection? The authors are an elementary/middle school librarian and a high school librarian who are developing ebook collections for their own libraries, and would like to share with other librarians the knowledge they have gleaned. A plethora of literature is available in journals and blogs, through conferences, webinars, and e-conferences. After combing through these resources, it became abundantly clear that a handbook would help others navigate the ebook waters.

When the writing process began for this book, there were few practical guides that focused on ebooks for school libraries. This book is for the neophyte who wants to begin developing an ebook collection, and the school librarian who has already started the process, but would appreciate some help with the next step.

Why write such a book when the ebook landscape is changing so rapidly that it seems at times impossible to pin anything down? We provide services to our students in this rapidly changing world and in the chaos of the now. We must not be paralyzed by the confusion that abounds. If we wait for the perfect computer with the fastest processor, largest memory, in the smallest size, we will never purchase a computer. In the same vein, if school librarians wait for the perfect ebook environment to arrive before starting the process of developing an ebook collection, they will be waiting a very long time, and students will not have the resources that they really need right now.

While developing the structure of this book, we discussed the processes that we had each used—and *wished* we had used—to acquire ebooks. The organization of this book is an extension of our discussions. Ebooks have become a popular book format, and they are a valuable educational resource.

Our goal is to facilitate your acquisition and familiarity with ebooks. We will examine their various formats and usage, provide an annotated list of vendors and devices to access ebooks from library collections, and also share some examples of collaboration with local public libraries. We will guide readers through the professional practices of purchasing, cataloging, and budgeting for e-resources, and discuss legal and ethical considerations.

What will the future bring for school library collections? We envision a world where library collections are a blend of print and digital resources. We are looking forward to the day when a book is just a book, when we can ask, "Have you read this wonderful title?" and the format will not be a factor. During a discussion of a great title, you won't hear anyone mention whether the book is hardback, paperback, audiobook, large print book, or an ebook. In preparation for that day, we need to acknowledge that ebooks are a valuable part of the resources we offer to our students.

What is an Ebook?

The ebook, electronic book, or digital book, is a young product that is constantly being revised, enhanced, and polished. Even the nomenclature has not been refined yet. One online search for ebooks produced four different variant terms and spellings: ebooks, eBooks, e-books, and digital books. This book will use the currently popular spellings "ebooks" and "Ebooks."

The *New Oxford American Dictionary* defines "e-book" as "an electronic version of a printed book that can be read on a computer or handheld device designed specifically for this purpose" (Oxford Univ. Press 2013). This book will focus on how ebooks can be used in schools, and how future changes will impact that use. First, let's take a look at how students and educators are currently using ebooks in libraries.

Usage Trends

Public libraries currently lead the way in ebook use. Circulation of ebooks at public libraries has soared in the past few years, quadrupling from 2010 to 2011. Over 90 percent of public libraries offer ebooks, and a third of those that don't are planning to do so soon. While adults aged 35 to 44 are the largest group of ebook readers through the public libraries, followed closely by those aged 45 to 54, the demographic with the largest increase over the past year was young adults/teens. A large majority (89 percent) of e-content accessed through public libraries last year was downloaded and then read offline; this finding differs greatly from what is found in academic and school libraries (School Library Journal 2012; Library Journal 2012a, 2012b).

In contrast, examination of school library use of ebooks shows a much more restrained adoption. As of 2012, only 40 percent of school libraries offered ebooks. This percentage is an increase over the 33 percent that offered ebooks in 2010, but the increase reflects very slow growth. If we break down school libraries by division, however, we find a livelier picture; 50 percent of middle school libraries offer ebooks, and fully 63 percent of upper school libraries do. This increase is mirrored by the increase in the size of ebook collections from elementary to high school. As size of collection increases with the grade level, so does circulation. Middle school circulation increased over that of elementary schools by 16 percent, while upper school circulation more than tripled. Oddly enough, ebook circulation at the elementary level was reduced by two-thirds between school year 2010–2011 and 2011–2012, indicating an unsettled horizon and highlighting the need to keep a weather eye out for unexpected shifts in practice (School Library Journal 2012).

Another factor influencing circulation data—and injecting an element of uncertainty into these statistics—is the fact that, for libraries whose materials are accessed online and are not downloaded, these items may not be considered to be "circulating," as students do not check out or download items, and often multiple users can access the material simultaneously. This is often the case with reference materials such as the Gale Virtual Reference Library (GVRL) and Humanities eBooks (ACLS-HEB). To obtain an accurate picture of usage of e-resources at a library, online-only usage statistics (which are usually available from vendors) must be included, along with circulation statistics. Circulation statistics relating to online materials must be gathered and read carefully to be sure of gaining an accurate indication of use.

Practically speaking, ebooks are used in schools in a variety of ways. Beyond the individual use by students, whether for recreational fiction or in the support of research papers, ebooks can be transformative when used in the classroom. Teachers at the Willows Community School in the Los Angeles area report success when working with ebooks and ebook apps in the classroom. Teachers like to project ebooks to an entire class for work with vocabulary on a class-wide scale, or to use the illustrations of a picture book as part of a lesson with younger readers. Language teachers also use ebooks to project to the whole class for work with translations. This is very handy as many ebooks are available in multiple languages. Students have also begun using the 'sample' function of an ebook to try an unfamiliar author out while at school or from home; if the student is intrigued then they may check out the ebook, or seek out the print version if they prefer that format. The ebook as an exploratory tool could increase the 'browsability' of the collection (Leverkus 2013).

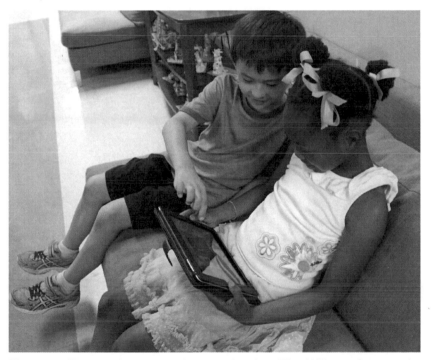

Figure 1. Two students enjoying an ebook at The Willows Community School.

Popularity of Types of Ebooks

Looking at the type of ebooks most in demand, public libraries report that the most commonly circulated ebooks in the fiction category were best sellers, mystery/suspense, romances, and general fiction. Most commonly circulated nonfiction ebooks were biography/memoir, best-selling nonfiction, and history, closely followed by self-help/psychology and political/current events (Library Journal 2012). Even though public libraries report best-selling fiction and nonfiction as top circulators, this usage is in spite of the difficulty libraries have in purchasing best sellers in digital format. The relationship with publishers is an area of continuing transition. Among others, the American Library Association (ALA), American Association of School Librarians (AASL), Authors for Library Ebooks, and Douglas County Libraries have been advocating for change with positive results.

Examination of popularity of types of ebooks in school libraries, not surprisingly, shows marked differences among grade levels. Elementary schools report their top circulating types as children's nonfiction, children's fiction, and children's picture books. Middle schools circulate mostly middle grade fiction, young adult fiction and middle grade nonfiction. High schools report their top circulating categories as reference ebooks, young adult fiction and young adult nonfiction (School Library Journal 2012).

Most school librarians expect the use of ebooks to continue to increase steadily in the future. Budgetary concerns are the number one issue librarians cite as limiting the growth of ebook use; the second issue mentioned most often, limited access to e-reading devices, is a financial issue as well. Also of concern is the lack of particular ebooks requested by students, and the limited number of titles offered. Librarians see that ebook use would be higher if more popular titles were made available to school libraries by publishers (School Library Journal 2012). See Chapter 8, Developing an Ebook Collection, for more on how students and educators use ebooks in the school library.

Ebooks are growing in popularity, and many companies are jumping into the ebook market with new formats, e-readers, and enhancements that will produce better ebooks and devices. The concept of the ebook has been around for a while, but it is really coming into its own as a 21st-century product. In fact, in the last thirteen years, more digital book types, formats, and devices have been developed than in the first sixty years of ebook history.

Ebook History

There is some debate about when ebooks were first invented. Various people have been credited with inventing the concept of the electronic book. Vannevar Bush, an American engineer and inventor, was the first person to clearly visualize a product similar to the ebooks that exist today. He imagined a desk that would display a book with distinct pages that could be turned, annotated, and stored on the desktop. It wasn't until 1965 that Ted Nelson, sociologist and information-technology pioneer, coined the words "hypertext" and "hypermedia." In 1968 Douglas Englebert at Stanford University designed the computer page, folders, and hypertext. Shortly after that Andries van Dam, Dutch-born computer science professor at Brown University, introduced a hypertext editing system (Gardner and Musto 2010, 165). Hypertext is text that links images, graphics, and text together using hyperlinks. The blue text on a webpage is a hyperlink, which, when selected, opens the connection to another page or graphic. "Most of the navigation features of ebooks are the result of hyperlinking, whether [to] the table of contents, annotations, cross references or bookmarks" (Gardner and Musto 2010, 167).

HyperCard was one of the first hypertext software packages offered as freeware on the Macintosh (Mac) computer in the late 1980s. By the early 1990s students were creating HyperCard presentations with pictures, graphs, charts, and other material linked to text. These HyperCard presentations were a precursor of the interactive ebooks or book apps available on so many different devices today (Leverkus 2013).

The early ebooks produced in the late 1980s and early 1990s were copied and sold on floppy disks, but these were bulky and difficult to read. The invention of the CD-ROM disk in the early 1990s offered the ebook publisher a better format that was easier to read. As Gardner and Musto mention in *The Oxford Companion to the Book*, "By 1992, the first e-book titles began to arrive on CD-ROM." Early ebooks available on CDs included the Bible and some reference works. The Library of Congress chose not to provide Cataloging in Publication (CIP) data for these ebook-CDs because they thought the format was too difficult to catalog and store. "The Library of Congress's decision not to catalogue CD-ROMs confirmed their end for all but large collections, archival use, or supplemental material in textbooks, instructors' manuals or study guides" (Gardner and Musto 2010, 166). Remember the *Britannica* and *World Book* CDs? The ability to search by keyword and find information through hyperlinks in the articles encouraged libraries to purchase these early CDs.

The next major invention that influenced the development of ebooks was the World Wide Web. In 1992, Marc Andreessen's team, working with the National Center for Supercomputing Applications, released Mosaic, the first Internet browser available to the general public. With Mosaic, which later morphed into Netscape, digital books could be accessed, downloaded, and read on the computer from any website (National Science Foundation n.d.). The early ebooks on the Web were typed or scanned into a computer and loaded onto a website. Later versions of ebooks added more features like hyperlinks and graphics.

Now ebooks use hypertext technology to access dictionaries, take notes, underline text, bookmark a page, or connect to narration for the text. These useful ebooks can be read in different formats on many kinds of devices such as smartphones, MP3 touch players, e-readers, and tablets.

With the introduction of the iPhone in 2007, touch screen technology was mass marketed. Applications displayed on the screen could be opened and manipulated with the touch of a finger. This latest technology transformed the market for electronic books. Later in 2007, the iPod touch was released as the first interactive MP3 player. In the next few years, many applications were developed with touch capability, including apps for reading books. Then, in 2010 Apple introduced the iPad with the proprietary iBooks app for reading ebooks from the iBook Store (Apple Inc. 2010). Book app developers realized that hypertext tools could be combined with touch technology to create engaging interactive books, which could be read on devices with touch screen technology. With the introduction of the iPad, book apps could be viewed on a larger screen. Within the first year after the iPad was introduced, the book app market was flooded with wonderful picture books that would intrigue any child or adult. In an article published by Library Media Connection Magazine, Cathy Leverkus describes some of the features of a book app, "*A Popout Peter*, displays something on every page that the reader can interact with. The owl hoots, Peter's sisters giggle; Mr. McGregor's sieve moves closer to Peter, or the blackberries burst when you touch them" (Leverkus 2011, 50). Microsoft, Samsung, Sony, and ASUS (manufacturer of Nexus tablets) are just a few of the companies that have developed many tablets with touch technology in the last couple of years.

Now the general population can create ebooks with programs like Apple iBooks Author and Adobe InDesign, which use hyperlinks to connect text, images, graphics, video, and other resources. Ebooks published with ebook-publishing programs can be read on most computers, tablets, MP3 touch players, smartphones, and e-readers such as the NOOK and Kindle. Self-published ebooks that are free or listed for a nominal price are becoming very popular at the ebook stores, and publishers are signing contracts with authors who have self-published their first works using ebook-publishing software. Online companies (such as PubIt! and Smashwords) that will publish ebooks for authors are covered in chapter 4.

Ebook Formats

Ebook companies like GVRL, ACLS-HEB, Apple, and Amazon use different ebook formats (ePub, HTML, PDF, plain text, and AZW) to add books to their collections. Sue Polanka (2013), in her webinar "Purchasing E-Books for Your Library," mentioned a useful Wikipedia article "Comparison of e-Book Formats" <http://en.wikipedia.org/wiki/Comparison_of_e-book_formats>. This resource can be used to study the capabilities of each format and to find out which devices can read the different formats (Wikimedia 2013a). Ebook publishers and vendors tend to use popular ebook formats. The most frequently used formats are described in this section (see table 1 for a list of vendors and formats).

HTML, Hypertext Markup Language, is used to create webpages. HTML is also used as a formatting language for ebooks. Tags indicate the configuration and design of the page, and determine the way the page is displayed. An HTML document begins with <HTML><Head> and then the topic of the document is entered, next the tag <BODY> precedes the text of the document, and, lastly, the document is concluded with </BODY>. Many tags exist that can be added to enhance the document. Other common tags identify hyperlinks, which direct readers to other webpages. For example, when creating ebooks with hypertext , clicking on the hyperlinked text "Chapter One" in the Table of Contents opens the text for chapter one (Refnes Data 2013).

Plain text (a TXT file), unlike HTML, does not contain hyperlinks or formatting commands and can be read without a reader app on any machine. Some self-published ebooks are created in plain text, which does not have a very attractive display. Spacing is not always consistent and graphics cannot be added to plain text (Sparks 2011).

AZW was one of the early formatting languages designed for Kindle e-readers. It is based on Mobipocket, formatting that was developed in France in 2000. Kindle Format 8 (**KF8**) was introduced in 2011 for the Kindle Fire line of ereaders. Because AZW and KF8 are proprietary formatting languages, ebooks published in these formats can be read only on the Kindle family of readers, which are currently Kindle, Kindle Fire, Kindle Fire HD, and Kindle Paperwhite (Wikimedia 2013a).

MOBI was designed in 2005 as a formatting language for mobile devices. The MOBI formatting language uses HTML tags to create ebook pages. Most of the major e-readers and all of the mobile devices (smartphones, tablets, and MP3/iPod touch) can download .mobi-formatted ebooks (Wikimedia 2013a).

The **ePub** (electronic publication) format is an open source standard format. In contrast to a proprietary formatting language that is developed for only one company's ereaders, an "open source standard format" means that it is publicly available. Ebooks published in

Table 1. Formats used by vendors to produce ebooks.

Vendor*	ePub	PDF	HTML	Plain text	Amazon AZW or KF8
ABC-Clio	yes	yes	yes	no	no
MackinVIA	yes	yes	yes	no	no
FollettShelf	yes	yes	yes	no	no
OverDrive	yes	yes	yes	no	yes
Brain Hive	yes	yes	yes	no	no
Axis 360	yes	yes	yes	no	no
GVRL [Gale Virtual Reference Library]	no	yes	yes	no	no
EBSCO	yes	yes	yes	no	no
Credo	no	yes	no	no	no
Proquest ebrary	yes	yes	yes	no	no
MyiLibrary	yes	yes	yes	no	no
3M Cloud	yes	yes	yes	no	no
Google Books	yes	yes	yes	yes	no
Project Gutenberg	yes	yes	yes	yes	yes

* Vendors are described in chapter 2.

Source: Information from vendors, Buffy Hamilton's webinar (2012) and Sue Polanka's webinar (2013).

ePub format can be read on most e-readers, tablets, and smartphones. International Digital Publishing Forum (IDPF) <http://idpf.org> the trade and standards organization of the digital-publishing industry, developed ePub formatting language in 2007. Many different ebook publishers quickly embraced ePub because it had more features than earlier formats and many different devices could be used to read a publisher's ebooks produced in ePub format. As mentioned on the IDPF website, "ePub publications, however, are designed to maximize accessibility for the visually impaired, and…typically perform text line layout and pagination on the fly, adapting to the size of the display area, the user's preferred font size, and other environmental factors." (IDPF 2012). In other words, with ePub's resizable font a full page of text will adjust to a smartphone, tablet, or a desktop screen without changing the font size or requiring the reader to scroll across the page. Some publications uploaded to the Internet are now being published in ePub format so the reader can take notes and copy content, instead of PDF format, which does not have these capabilities.

iBook formatting language was created by Apple for the ebook-building program iBook Author. It is a proprietary format based on the ePub standard. Ironically, books purchased from the iBookstore and read on the iBook app are in ePub format.

2

Sources of Ebooks

School librarians have a variety of options to choose from for adding digital content to school library collections, including purchasing or licensing ebooks from ebook vendors and publishers, or adding hyperlinks to the school website to free ebook websites and public library digital collections. A school library that has not yet added e-content to its collection might want to direct students to free ebook websites and digital content at public libraries as a first step. After students have had time to use these free collections, school librarians can assess the curricular needs of the school and start adding ebook content to the library collection. Additionally, a school library with existing e-collections may desire to add more digital resources after reviewing the products in this chapter.

Ebook Vendors

Ebook vendors develop platforms to read, display, and access digital content. Each vendor has created a unique platform for displaying

> License agreements must be read very carefully before a librarian commits to a particular program or ebook platform for a school library.

e-content. The intended audience and the type of ebook both influence the platform design. A platform for young readers is simple to navigate and very colorful; one used for searching a nonfiction collection for middle school or high school research will be more utilitarian but still quite colorful. Vendor websites explain the product, identify the intended audience and provide contact information. All vendors will set-up trials and connect libraries with sales reps that can answer any questions about their product.

Vendors have various pricing models. The term "purchase" when used by commercial digital book companies and vendors refers to buying a license. Amazon, Barnes & Noble, Sony, Kobo, e-textbook companies, ebook vendors and many ebook publishers do not sell their ebooks; they sell a license to access them. However, some of the vendors and commercial digital book companies sell ebooks with long-term license agreements. If librarians decide to change ebook vendors, many of these companies will help move their product to another platform. Other companies do not cooperate with buyers who change vendors; in these cases, if a librarian decides to change vendors, the library patrons loose access to all of the ebooks that have been purchased. License agreements must be read very carefully before a librarian commits to a particular program or ebook platform for a school library. Although most ebooks are distributed under a licencing agreement, a few ebook publishers, and some authors will sell their ebooks directly to libraries. Libraries can also purchase author's ebooks through vendor/distributors like Smashwords.

Douglas County Libraries (DCL) has built a platform for ebooks that the library system has purchased from publishers and authors (DCL 2012a). Building on DCL's open source platform, Califa Library Group, a consortium of California libraries has developed Enki Library to host ebook content. Califa members, beginning with Contra Costa County Library and San Francisco Public Library, have access to this ebook collection (Enis 2013a). You can read more about these programs in chapter 10.

Commercial Ebooks

Reading ebooks on a laptop or desktop is useful for research projects, but cuddling up with a desktop or laptop to read a favorite fiction story is cumbersome. Decision makers at companies that were selling ebooks realized that they needed to sell a device that was lightweight, had a clean display, and was simple to use for reading ebooks. The e-reader, a compact device, was the solution. A few of the major companies that developed e-readers for their ebook collections were Sony, Amazon, Barnes & Noble (B&N), Kobo, and Apple.

Alex Sharp posted a blog about e-reader history which refered to articles in the *The New York Times*, *Wired*, and *Times Daily*. She mentioned, that Barnes & Noble began selling ebooks in 1998, and "Rocket eBook: the first e-reader" entered the market that same year. Sharp said, "The [Rocket eBook] company was sold" in 2003 when Barnes & Noble stopped selling ebooks. Barnes & Noble felt ebooks were not a profitable product (Sharp 2010).

The US Guradian published an ebook timeline, which mentioned an agreement between Microsoft and Amazon in 2000. "The online bookstore used the new Microsoft software to enable customers to download their ebooks on to PCs and handhelds" (Ebook Timeline 2001). Now Amazon was able to sell ebooks that could be read on PCs, Palm Pilots and PDA's. In 2001, four of the major publishers added ebooks to their product line including: Time Warner, Penguin, Random House and HarperCollins. In December of the same year Time Warner closed the ebook publishing unit ipublish, stating that: "The market for ebooks has simply not developed the way we hoped" (Ebook Timeline 2001). Amazon was one of the few companies that continuously sold ebooks throughout the early growth of the ebook industry. The Amazon Kindle and Sony Reader were introduced in 2007, and B&N introduced the Nook in 2009. By the end of 2009, e-readers and ebooks were well on their way to becoming the popular products they are today.

These commercial companies do not provide MARC records for the ebooks they sell. A circulating e-reader and any ebooks on the e-reader will need to be cataloged so students and faculty can view the titles in the ebook collection. Circulating an e-reader loaded with ebooks does have one major drawback; none of the titles on that e-reader are available to other patrons when the device is checked-out. It is also questionable whether circulating the e-readers loaded with ebooks is advisable. More information about circulating loaded e-readers can be found in chapter 14. Cataloging is addressed in chapter 11.

Publisher's Sales Policies for Libraries

Sales departments at large publishing firms are trying to figure out how to profit from ebook sales to libraries. Consequently, they are instituting new sales policies for library ebook purchases. In 2013, Random House tripled the price of the ebooks sold to libraries. HarperCollins' purchase policy limits libraries to twenty-six circulations per title; to continue to circulate the title, it must be purchased again for another twenty-six loans (Kelley 2012). "Hachette offers a portion of its backlist at increased prices," and Macmillan began selling backlist Minotaur imprint titles for two years or fifty-two loans per title (Milliot 2013). Anthony W. Marx, President of the New York Public Library commented in an opinion piece for *The New York Times* that Simon & Schuster has recently started a pilot program to sell ebooks to New York City libraries (Marx 2013). Simon and Schuster has chosen to circulate the ebooks through the 3M Cloud Library and Baker and Taylor Axis 360 platforms. They have not established the price they will charge libraries for ebooks after the pilot program has ended, but one of the pilot requirements is that the library patrons will have the options to either check out the ebooks or purchase them. (Vinjamuri 2013).

Penguin changed their library sales policy quite a few times in 2012 and the beginning of 2013. A blog on the Digital Book World site reported that, "for about six months in 2012, Penguin wasn't selling ebooks to libraries at all; in February it had cut ties with library ebook distributor OverDrive." Later on that month they stopped selling ebooks to all libraries…In the Summer, [Penguin] started a pilot [program] with the New York Public Library [through] ebook library distributor 3M", and Los Anglels Public Library (LAPL) through Axis 360. In October, the company rolled out its ebook program to all of 3M's 70 or so library systems across the U.S. However, the program had stipulations…Penguin required a six month waiting period for libraries on newly released ebooks. Additionally, ebook copies would expire after a year and librarians who wanted to continue to stock the titles would have to re-purchase them (Report 2013). This new policy of waiting six months to sell ebooks to libraries was reffered to as "windowing." Librarians boycotted Penguin because of windowing. Subsequently, Penguin dropped their windowing policy in March of 2013. Penguin has recently merged with Random House to create Penguin Random House. At the time of publication the new company had not yet published their sales policies for ebooks. See more about Penguin in chapter 15.

ALA's Response to Publisher Ebook Policy

Now, all big six publishers are engaged in selling ebooks to libraries to some extent, but title selection can be limited and pricing prohibitive. Maureen Sullivan, ALA president 2012–2013, has stated, "If our libraries' digital bookshelves mirrored *The New York Times* fiction best seller list, we would be missing half of our collection any given week due to these publishers' policies" (Sullivan 2012). Librarians need an advocate to negotiate with the publishers, and Sullivan has commented, "We have established ALA as an important player in addressing the various issues around the changes in the digital content ecosystem" (2013). Eventually, publishers will need to develop a library ebook sales policy that both sellers and buyers believe is reasonable. In the ALA press releases for June 27, 2013 it was stated that, "Today, Maureen Sullivan, president of the American Library Association (ALA), announced the launch of 'Authors for Library Ebooks,' a new initiative that asks authors to stand with libraries in their quest for equitable access to e-books. Bestselling authors Cory Doctorow, Ursula K. Le Guin and Jodi Picoult are helping kick off the campaign…[The] Authors for Library E-books campaign encourages authors to sign on to a statement of shared values, to discuss the issue with their publishers, and raise awareness of their concerns through their websites, social media and other communications channels" (ALA 2013a). Now noted authors are working with ALA to encourage publishers to develop reasonable sales policies and vendors are also working with publishers to encour-

Table 2. What does each publisher offer?

Hachette Book Group	Full catalog, released simultaneously with print; ebooks will cost 300 percent more than the print book; unlimited number of checkouts; one copy per user model.
Simon & Schuster	Started a one year pilot project on April 30 with New York Public Library, Brooklyn Public Library, and the Queens Library. Offering full catalog; one-year purchase/license; unlimited checkouts; one copy per user model.
MacMillan Publishers	1,200 backlist ebooks from its Minotaur Books imprint; two-year, 52 lends license model; ebooks cost $25; still in pilot project mode.
Random House	Our ebook friends, for a price—entire catalogue available for "perpetual access" at a higher price to libraries (upwards of 300% over the print book cost).
Penguin	All titles available; one-year licenses, except if you're OverDrive.
HarperCollins	26 check-outs per title license model.

Source: Information from a David Lee King blog post, "The Big Six: Where We Stand At The Moment" (King 2013).

age them to make more titles available to libraries. Positive change is inevitable. Librarians must watch the media for the latest news about publishers and libraries. Sources of news about ebooks and e-publishing are in chapter 13, chapter 16, and Appendix A. The sales policies for the Big Six publishers as of June 16, 2013 are listed in table 2.

Vendors as Library Publisher Liasons

It would be a huge job for librarians to keep track of all the different ebook policies that publishers have instituted. They would have to record the number of check-outs or the length of time the ebook was in circulation. Luckily, the vendors keep track of all this information, and they will notify the library when a book needs to be repurchased.

Michael Bills, director of digital products sales at Baker & Taylor, described how the vendors assist school libraries with the different publisher sales policies. "Baker & Taylor manages usage rights for both circ-based or time-limited access to titles according to publishers' terms of sales for libraries. Usage tracking in the Axis 360 system allows B&T to send email notifications to libraries alerting them that copies are nearing their access limits. Libraries may re-purchase copies to maintain access." If libraries choose to not repurchase tites, "the copies that have reached their circulation limits are deactivated and removed from the library's Axis 360 repository" (Bills 2013). Repurchasing does give library staff the opportunity to determine if a title should be left in a collection. The school librarian will want to evaluate the usage statistics and curriculum needs before deciding whether to repurchase a title.

Ebook Vendors

Ebook vendors design platforms and e-reading applications to deliver ebooks from the various publishers to readers. Many of the vendors mentioned in this section prepare MARC (Machine-Readable Cataloging) records for any titles purchased; as a result, libraries can easily add these records to their integrated library systems (ILS). With the addition of these records, a school library's ILS can search all the ebook and print resources available to students and faculty.

Elementary and Middle School Vendors

BookFlix <http://teacher.scholastic.com/products/bookflixfreetrial/index.htm> is a subscription service that pairs video storybooks with Scholastic nonfiction ebooks for K–3 readers. Definitions and narration are built into all of the Scholastic BookFlix ebooks. Scholastic provides MARC records for the econtent, and students can access the resources with any device that connects to the Internet. BookFlix also offers Spanish-language ebooks and videos. (Scholastic 2013).

StarWalk Kids Media <www.starwalkkids.com/about-us/our-mission.html> was developed by Seymour Simon to offer quality ebooks for elementary and middle school students. The company consistently adds new titles to the collection each year. "Every eBook in the StarWalk Kids catalog has been evaluated and matched to appropriate Common Core State Standards. The accompanying 'Teaching Links' document suggests approaches and activities to enhance [Common Core State Standards] related learning for that specific book" (Seymour Science 2012). The ebook collection of around two hundred fiction and nonfiction titles showcases works by award-winning authors. All the titles are narrated, and contain highlighting and note-taking tools. The Starwalk website notes that, "institutional subscriptions start at $595 for a single location" (Seymour Science 2013). All the ebooks in the StarWalk collection have unlimited simultaneous access. Unlimited simultaneous access permits all of the students in a school to have complete acces to all the ebooks on tablets, laptops, and desktop computers.

K–12 Vendors

Capstone Digital <www.capstonepub.com/content/DIGITAL_CIL> is not a subscription service. Capstone Digital sells interactive picture books and graphic novels (with natural-voice audio) for emergent and reluctant readers. Capstone Interactive Library platform for K–8 students includes over two thousand enhanced ebooks and graphic novels (Capstone 2011a). The MyON platform has more than three thousand enhanced digital books for K–12 students; the books can be assigned to students by Lexile level and reading interest (Capstone 2011c). Capstone ebooks offer unlimited simultaneous access so all of the students at a school can access the ebooks at the same time. The Capstone digital resources can be read on laptops and desktops. They recently add an iPad app. (Capstone 2011b).

TumbleBookLibrary <www.tumblebooks.com> includes four different collections of videos, graphic novels, audiobooks, and games. The early-elementary collection of animated talking picture books and chapter books that includes TumbleGames is TumbleBookLibrary. TumbleBookLibrary can be accessed through the website or it can be downloaded from a fully loaded USB flash drive to be read offline. For upper-elementary students, a collection of ebooks, graphic novels, audiobooks, and National Geographic videos can be found on the TumbleBookCloud Junior platform. The middle school and high school platform TumbleBookCloud features two separate collections: a middle school collection and a high school collection of core curriculum materials, recreational reading, and graphic novels. All the books in the TumbleBookCloud collections are also narrated. TheTumbleBookLibrary platforms are available through a yearly subscription (TumbleBookLibrary n.d.).

Brain Hive <www.brainhive.com/Pages/Home.aspx> is a relatively new K–12 ebook platform with an unique pricing formula. This vendor charges $1 for each book circulated from the collection. Because the subscription is paid for by the charge per rental of each ebook, setting a spending ceiling for this product is very important — $1 per book can add up quickly! Brain Hive does keep track of the rentals and will alert the school when a budget limit has been reached. The Brain Hive platform offers ebooks for emergent readers and young adults, as well as some adult titles. Each Brain Hive account has an account administrator (a member of the library staff) who can delete access to any titles that are not geared for the grade levels at the school. According to a member of the Brain Hive technical support team, libraries have the option of purchasing a long-term lease for high-circulation ebooks, if the publisher agrees to lease the ebook (Snell 2013). The 3,000+ ebooks can be read on any laptop, desktop, Android, or iOS device (Brain Hive 2013).

Smashwords <www.smashwords.com> is a publisher/distributor/ vendor of Digital Right Management (DRM) free indie books. DRM free means the ebooks can be transferred to different devices and the publisher or vendor will not pull them from your e-reader. More information about DRM is in chapter 8 and chapter 14. Smashwords offers three options for accesing the ebooks. The books can be purchased directly from the website and loaded on a personal e-reader (iPad, Kindle, Sony eReader, NOOK, KOBO, smartphone or tablet), read at the website in your personal library of ebooks, or accessed through another publisher or vendor that has purchased ebooks from Smashwords for their platform. The headline for an article on Smashwords in Forbes

Magazine was, "Apple's Biggest (Unknown) Supplier of E-Books" (Colao 2012). On the Smashwords website, founder Mark Coker wrote, "Smashwords provides an opportunity to discover new voices in all categories and genres of the written word. Once you register, the site offers useful tools for search, discovery, and a library-building platform. Most of our books are affordably priced, and many are free" (Smashwords, Inc. 2013). There is a large selection of children's books at the website and Smashwords' website offers an adult filter so librarians can limit adult content on the library platform. They offer over 125,000 ebooks from 50,000 authors and indie publishers in ePub, PDF, AZW and HTML formats. Choose ebooks from a self-publishing firm carefully. An editor has not monitored the publishing process, and therefore the quality of the books is inconsistent.

FollettShelf <www.aboutfollettebooks.com/follettshelf.cfm> is the platform used to store and access the collection of over 145,000 ebooks that can be purchased from Follett. Also, content from other ebook vendors can be read on FollettShelf. ABDO Digital Databases, Capstone Interactive Library, Lerner Interactive Books, PebbleGo, Rosen's PowerKnowledge Science Suite, Rosen's Teen Health & Wellness, Rourke Interactive eBooks, and TumbleBook are some of the vendor and publisher platforms that are available through Follett. These ebooks can be read on laptops, desktops, smartphones, and iPads. The platform offers note taking and highlighting features. Also, the latest version of the FollettShelf Digital Reader Textflow app allows patrons to access the ebooks from their account via the cloud. With this new app, books can be read on different devices during the checkout period (Follett 2013). According to Follett, vendor representatives will help set up patron accounts for the different reading levels at the school. Follett does not charge a hosting fee to use this ebook platform.

Baker & Taylor (B&T) created the **Axis 360 platform** <http://btol.com/axis360> to showcase ebooks and audiobooks. The ebooks, available in both ePub and PDF formats, can be read on tablets, smartphones, iPods, NOOKs, Sony Readers, Kobo e-readers, and the Kindle Fire and Kindle HD. B & T ebooks can also be read with the Blio e-reader app, which offers many features, such as text-to-speech, smooth page turn, white text on black background, note

Figure 2. Baker & Taylor ebook platform.

taking, dictionary, and encyclopedia access. In July 2012 the National Federation of the Blind honored Axis 360 for providing a platform that was easily accessible with enriched audio content and white text on black background for the sight-impaired.

Axis 360 charges a yearly platform-hosting fee of $250, which is used to update and maintain the platform. Michael Bills, director of digital products sales at Baker & Taylor stated that, "purchases for Axis 360 are portable. The publishers [that Baker & Taylor work with] do not sell the actual ebook files; they sell a license to access the content. Baker & Taylor considers that license to be permanent. If any Axis 360 library elects to change platforms we will work with them and the e-content suppliers to secure permission for the library to transfer their access license to their new platform" (2013).

OverDrive <www.overdrive.com> has a large collection of over one million ebooks, including public domain works that can be read on any Android or iOS device and e-reader, including the Kindle line. OverDrive offers their patrons ease of access and a large collection of titles. Laura Ruttig, an account executive at OverDrive, wrote "Our full catalog (including adult bestsellers, university press titles for colleges & universities, and other mature titles) contains over 1,000,000 e-books, digital audiobooks, music, and video files. Of that, ~350,000 have been designated by publishers as specifically geared towards the K–12 market" (Ruttig 2013). These 350,000 titles are not necessarily just for school libraries. There are many titles that would be a nice addition to an adult collection such as *Farenheit 451*. Schools are welcome to choose any of the 1,000,000 digital titles available. They are not limited to the titles selected for the K–12 market. "The OverDrive service involves an annual fee that includes the platform fee and content acquisition credits" (Burleigh 2013). Fifty-percent of the fee is for hosting the books on the OverDrive platform and the other 50 percent is used as content credit to build the collection. They offer various options for single schools as well as special district pricing. David Burleigh Director of Marketing stated that OverDrive offers "a variety of access models ranging from one-copy-per-user to simultaneous access" (2013). OverDrive is similar to other platforms such as ACLS-HEB and TumbleCloudLibrary. There is a yearly fee to continue using the platform. According to the OverDrive school license agreement, "access to SDL [School Download Library] service shall be for a period of twelve (12) consecutive months starting the effective date of service launch" (OverDrive, Inc. 2013).

3M Cloud Library <http://3m-ssd.implex.net/cloudapps/index.html> not only lends ebooks, it also sells e-readers for circulating the ebooks, and electronic podiums (3M Discovery Terminals) for searching the 3M Cloud Library and checking out books. Although purchase of the e-reader or terminal to use 3M's digital library is not required, these are options that offer instantaneous access to all the ebooks in the library collection (Monson 2012). Other ebook vendors originally sold print books and then, when ebooks became a desired product, they added ebooks to their merchandise line. 3M developed the e-reader first and then created the ebook collection. 3M Cloud Library started offering its platform to libraries in 2012. Katie Bane stated in an American Libraries article published, May 14, 2012 that, "after several months of beta testing, 3M has launched the 3M Cloud Library eBook Lending Service" (2012). 3M is one of the youngest companies in the ebook lending field and already has over 200,000 ePub ebooks available for computers, most e-readers, and iOS and Android devices. Penguin has begun a limited library lending policy with 3M at NYPL, which is the same as the arrangement between Penguin and Axis 360. Both vendors will begin adding Penguin Random House ebooks to their platforms soon.

Nonfiction Research Ebook Collections

The platforms described below function like databases that search the contents of the ebook collection. Students can search by subject or keyword to find information for their research projects. They can also download information to the computer or print sections of the ebooks. These platforms offer useful tools such as highlighting and note taking along with dictionary and encyclopedia access.

Content Management Platform

MackinVIA <www.mackin.com/eServices/MACKIN-VIA.aspx> has a large collection of nonfiction ebooks that are available to read on the MackinVIA platform, which includes a basic keyword subject search engine. In 2012 fiction titles were added to the ebook content. MackinVIA can manage some of the electronic resources to which a library subscribes or has purchased a license; these resources include: databases, journals, newspapers, and ebooks. Mackin does not charge a hosting fee for the platform; the company has a license agreement for ebooks published by ABC-CLIO, ABDO, Britannica, Capstone Interactive, Gale, and Infobase Publishing, as well as titles from some other publishers. Mackin offers over 100,000 ebooks. They recently developed mobile platforms for the iPad, Kindle, NOOK and Android tablets; and desktop platforms for the MAC and Windows operating systems. Check with Mackin to make sure they support the databases, journals, newpapers and ebooks in the libary e-collections.

Mackin, *School Library Journal* and the Genesee Valley Educational

Partnership created the website "Here Be Fiction" <www.herebefiction. org/> where school librarians can peruse reviews of quality fiction. The website offers single user and multiuser license options, and the ebooks can be accessed from the MackinVIA platform. This is a valuable tool for school librarians (Harris 2013b). More information about the "Here Be Fiction" website can be found in chapters 13 and 15.

EBSCOhost ebook collections <www.ebscohost.com/ebooks> offer various purchase options. Libraries can subscribe to an ebook bundle with unlimited simultaneous access; fill a student's request with a short-time loan; or purchase a long-term lease for individual titles with single-user access, three-user simultaneous access, or unlimited simultaneous access. EBSCOhost also offers a package that will manage a library's e-resources through the EBSCOhost platform using EBSCO Discovery Services (EBSCO Industries, Inc. 2012). More information about EBSCO Discovery Services can be found in chapter 7.

Nonfiction Collections

ProQuest ebrary/EBL <www.proquest.com/en-US/products/brands/ pl_ebrary.shtml>, ProQuest recently purchased **Ebook Library (EBL)** <http://www.eblib.com/?p=index>. The merger will combine the assets of both EBL and ebrary platforms, expanding the content available to users. The EBL platform adds superior search capabilities to ebrary, which offers over 75,000 titles as a subscription, and access to 120,000 other titles through either patron driven access, short-term loans or long-term licenses. The merger seems to favor the use of the EBL platform.

Ebrary has developed an ebook platform concept for high schools in which a majority of the e-titles are acquired through a subscription, a few titles can be added as short term loans, and other options are a long-term license using either patron driven access or adding a "perpetual archive" title. "Perptual archive" is the term ebrary uses to describe the e-titles acquired with their long-term license agreement (ebrary n.d.) More information about acquisition models can be found in Chapter 9.

American Council Of Learned Sociaties-Humanities E-Book (ACLS-HEB) <http://humanitiesebook.org/about-us/default.html>

is a subscription service of 3,500 humanities ebooks. Each year HEB adds hundreds of new titles to the collection. The ACLS website states that, "these titles are offered by ACLS in collaboration with twenty-seven learned societies, over 100 contributing publishers, and the MPublishing Division of the University of Michigan Library...The collection features unlimited multi-user access and free, downloadable MARC records" (ACLS Humanities E-book).

Credo <corp.credoreference.com/index.php> has four ebook collections: Literati School, Academic, Credo online Reference Service, and Student Athlete. The Two e-collections that high schools subscribe to are Literati School and Credo Online Reference Service. The Literati School core collection contains ebooks from forty-six different publishers including Penguin, Dorling Kindersley, ABC-CLIO, and Encyclopaedia Britannica. The Credo website states that, "collections can be added to your Literati School subscription or acquired separately under both subscription and perpetual access models" (Credo. n.d. a). Perpetual access is purchasing a long-term license agreement for each title. Credo Online Reference Service features publisher collections such as ABC-CLIO's Contemporary World Issues a selection of seventy-five resources on biological warfare, climate change, and conflicts over natural resources, etc. This is only one example of the forty-six different collections available through Online Reference Service (Credo n.d.-b). Any computer, tablet or phone with Internet access can search the school library Credo ebook collection.

Gale Virtual Reference Library Platform (GVRL) <www.gale. cengage.com/servlet/GvrlMS?msg=ma> charges a nominal hosting fee of $50 a year for access to a large collection of nonfiction ebooks. All the GVRL titles have unlimited simultaneous access with long-term license agreements. GVRL is a virtual reference platform (see figure 3) that offers many useful Gale resources as well as e-titles from other publishers (Vidal 2013). Over one hundred and twenty publishers including Dorling Kindersley, ABC-CLIO, Facts on File, Oxford University Press, and Encyclopaedia Britannica publish ebooks available on the GVRL platform. The company that developed GVRL — Gale Cengage Learning — also offers quality databases designed to support K–12 curriculum.

JSTOR <http://books.jstor.org>, known for its academic periodical collection, offers over fourteen thousand ebooks — most from academic presses — that can be aquired with either a single-user or unlimited simultaneous user license. The JSTOR platform can be used to search both the ebooks and periodicals in a school's JSTOR collection (ITHAKA 2012).

Ingram MyiLibrary <www.myilibrary.com>, a nonfiction ebook library platform for school, public, and professional libraries, has a flexible purchasing model. JSTOR also offers a similar model for purchasing ebooks. The MyiLibrary Features webpage describes the "flexible sales options: title-by-title or full collection, in perpetuity or by subscription. Includes unique offerings such as inter-library e-loans and multiple pricing options such as buying across publishers or subject areas" (MyiLibrary n.d.). Also, both JSTOR and Ingram promote demand-driven acquisition. A library can select a title for the

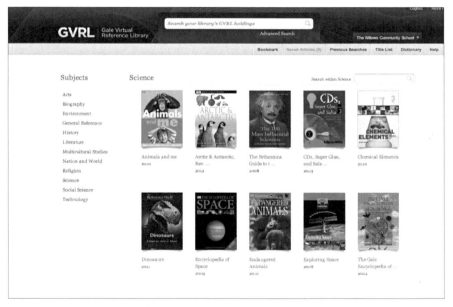

Figure 3. Example of GVRL user interface for a K-8 school. From Gale. *Gale Virtual Reference Library.* © Gale, a part of Cengage Learning, Inc. Reproduced by permission. www.cengage.com/ permissions.

collection, but it is not purchased until a specified number of patrons access the title. Information about different acquisition models can be found in chapter 9.

Additional Sources of Nonfiction

ABC-CLIO <http://ebooks.abc-clio.com/main.aspx> has published more than 7,000 single title ebooks, and professional development resources such as library journals, online lesson plans and webinars. ABC-CLIO also publishes database textbooks, including *American Government*, *American History*, *Pop Culture* and others. This concept of the database and textbook meddled together is a format that other publishers are developing.

The **Salem Press** <http://salempress.com/store/pages/ebooks. htm> sales representative described an alternative program that offers access to the Salem databases when you purchase a print book. "If you purchase one of our print titles that includes online access to the same content on one of our databases, you have access to the online content until a revised or new edition [of the book] is published. If you purchase our content in ebook format, our ebooks are hosted on EBSCOhost" (Cabiness 2013).

The Publishers **Rosen** <www.rosenpublishing.com>, **Infobase** <www.infobasepublishing.com> (Facts on File and Chelsea House), **Britannica** < http://eb.pdn.ipublishcentral.com>, **Scholastic** <http:// store.scholastic.com/landing-page/landingpage/storia/shop-ebooks>, **Capstone**, **ABC-CLIO**, **Oxford** <www.oxford-ebooks.com/ oe2/index.php>, and **Salem** offer ebooks that libraries can acquire directly from the publishers. Library patrons can read the ebooks on the publishers' ebook platforms. Or, these publisher's ebooks can be purchsed through vendors. The ebooks issued by the aforementioned publishers are available on vendor platforms such as MackinVIA, Axis 360, EBSCOhost, FollettShelf, MyiLibrary, ProQuest ebrary, Gale's GVRL, and ACLS-HEB. Using individual publisher platforms to access ebooks can be difficult, because the librarian would have more ebook platforms to administer. Purchasing a license for the publishers' books from large vendors creates less work for librarians.

Comparison of Platforms

Table 3. Platform comparison chart provides a comparison and overview of the major suppliers of ebooks to libraries.

Platform	License/Subscribe/Rent	Reference Tools (See Note 1)	Notetaking	Searchable Text	Hosting Fee	Individual or Unlimited Simultaneous Access (USA)	E-readers (See Note 2)
TumbleBookLibrary	subscribe	no	no	no	no	USA	iOS and Android
TumbleBookCloud	subscribe	no	yes	no	no	USA	iOS and Android
StarWalk	subscribe	no	yes	yes	no	USA	iOS
Capstone	subscribe	no	no	no	no	USA	iOS and Android
BookFlixs	subscribe	yes	no	no	no	USA	desktop and laptop only
MackinVIA	license	yes	yes	yes	no	individual; some titles USA	iOS and Android
FollettShelf	license	no	yes	yes	no	individual; some titles USA	iOS and Android
OverDrive	subscribe to a customized collection	yes iOS and Android	yes	yes	no	individual; some titles USA	iOS, Android, NOOK, Kindle, Kobo, Sony
Brain Hive	rental: pay $1 for each check-out or lease	no	yes	no	no	USA	iOS and Android
Smashwords (See Note 3)	purchase DRM free	yes	yes (depending on reader)	yes (depending on reader)	yes (depending on reader)	individual	iOS, Android, NOOK, Kindle, Kobo, 3M
B&T Axis 360	license	yes iOS and Android	yes	yes	yes	individual; some titles USA	iOS, Android, NOOK, Kindle Fire, Kobo, Sony
3M Cloud	license	no	yes	yes	yes	individual	iOS, Android, NOOK, Kindle Fire, Kobo, Sony, 3M

ABC-CLIO	license	yes	yes	yes	no	Individual	iOS and Android
Credo	license and subscribe options	yes	yes	yes	no	USA	tablets, computers, smartphones
JSTOR ebooks	subscribe to a customized collection or bundled collection	yes	yes	yes	no	USA	iOS and Android
ACLS-HEB	subscribe	no	yes	yes	no	USA	desktop and laptop only
GVRL	license	yes	yes	yes	yes	USA	iOS and Android
EBSCO	license or subscribe to customized collection or bundled collection	yes	yes	yes	no	individual; many titles USA	iOS and Android
ProQuest ebrary	subscribe to collections	yes	yes	yes	no	USA	iOS and Android
MyiLibrary	license or subscribe to customized collection or bundled collection	yes	yes	yes	no	USA	iOS and Android

Note 1: Reference tools are dictionaries and encyclopedias.

Note 2: All platforms can be accessed and content read on desktops and laptops.

Note 3: Smashwords books can be read with many different reader apps. The tools available depend on which app is chosen to read the ebook.

Note 4: Vendors are constantly adding new apps and formatting languages to create access for more e-readers and other devices.

Source: Information from vendors and vendor websites.

Results of Ebook Usage Survey

A survey of ebook collections and ebook usage was completed by 105 members of the Association of Independent School Librarians (AISL). Of the respondents, 87 answered the question "What Vendor or Vendors do you purchase your ebooks from?" (Leverkus and Acedo 2012). Their responses are listed in table 4.

Table 4. AISL Member Survey of eBook Vendor Use (Individual refers to individual publishers)

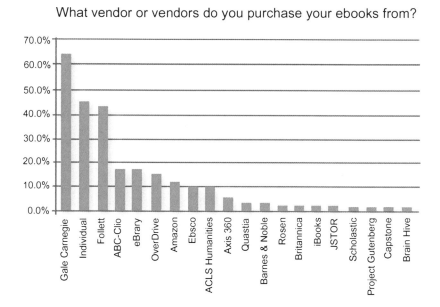

What vendor or vendors do you purchase your ebooks from?

Free Ebook Websites

Free ebooks that can be downloaded to students' e-readers or read on their computers and laptops are available at quite a few websites. The websites mentioned in this section have been selected because they offer quality products and a large selection of titles. Some of the websites listed below may also sell ebooks, but their free ebook collections are quite large. A link on a library's webpage to these sites would enhance the library's ebook collection and provide free ebooks to patrons. On-line access — or reading an ebook directly from the website on a laptop, desktop or other device — is a common form of access for these sites. More about online access can be found in Chapter 6.

ManyBooks.net <http://manybooks.net> is a website that offers approximately 29,000 free ebooks that can be played on most devices. This collection is gathered from Project Gutenberg, public domain titles and creative commons works (ManyBooks.net n.d.).

Feedbooks <www.feedbooks.com> based in Paris, France, is an ebook retailer that also distributes a large collection of public domain ebooks in ePub format. Ebooks created in ePub format can be read on most e-readers. This site's English-language public domain collection is quite extensive and includes: The Harvard Classics, public domain titles that are on reading lists for U.S. high schools, noteworthy banned books, and Encyclopedia Britannica's Great Books of the Western World (Feedbooks 2013).

International Children's Digital Library <http://en.childrenslibrary.org> began operations in 2002 with the goal of distributing free ebooks of tales from around the world. Presently, the ICDL collection contains almost five thousand ebooks in sixty-one languages (International Children's Digital Library 2013). The ICDL offers an app for downloading and reading the titles on iOS devices. Apple's iOS is the operating system for the iPhone and iPad.

Kobo <www.kobobooks.com> offers over one million free ebooks. Kobo is a subsidiary of Rakuten, Japan's largest digital-products company. The ebooks can be read on most devices through the Kobo apps for iOS and Android (Google's touch screen operating system). Kobo also sells ebooks and Kobo e-readers. Their ebooks are available in many languages, because the collection is composed of books published in over 170 countries (Kobo, Inc. n.d.-a).

Rare Book Room <http://rarebookroom.org> was developed as a collection of high-quality digital photographs of the world's greatest literature. Octavo, a digital photography firm, has photographed around four hundred books that can be accessed at this site. Shakespeare, Benjamin Franklin, Galileo, Aesop, Lewis Carroll, and Copernicus are just a few of the great authors, scientists, and inventors whose works are included in this digital library. Each page is a high-quality digital photograph (Rare Book Room n.d.).

The Library of Congress <http://archive.org/details/library_of_congress> has digital content that can be accessed on The Library of Congress Archive webpage, but only a small portion of the collection has been digitized. The Library of Congress' virtual programs & services webpage describes the perameters of the collection, "[the] available full-text [ebooks] are mostly American publications published prior to 1923, which are no longer under U.S. copyright protection. Academic textbooks and recent works of fiction cannot be found in full-text/electronic formats…" (The Library of Congress 2011). The nonfiction e-collection largely contains Library of Congress publications. Three different e-collections are available at The Library of Congress website. "American Memory", contains over 1,200 e-resources including books, maps, images, and manuscripts. "The Global Gateway" collection focuses on world culture and history. And, The Sloan Foundation supports a program which "scans and digitizes public domain works, with a major focus on at-risk brittle books and U.S. history volumes" found in The Library of Congress collection (The Library of Congress 2012).

Large Digitized Collections of Free Ebooks

The large collections of free ebooks, Project Gutenberg, Google Books, World Digital Library, HathiTrust, and Digital Public Library of America (DPLA), all have a similar goal: to produce a digital copy of books and other primary resources that have been locked away in special libraries, and make them available to the world. Many of the works included in these collections are now in the public domain; therefore, the entire resource can be copied and added to these projects.

Project Gutenberg <www.gutenberg.org> began as a volunteer crowd-sourced effort to digitize cultural works in 1971. The early Project Gutenberg books were laboriously typed by hand on a computer and uploaded to the website. Portable Document Format (PDF) was developed in the early 1990s. With the advent of PDF, books could be scanned into computers, converted to PDF files, and uploaded to the Internet. A PDF file will preserve the original font and illustrations or images. Later, Project Gutenberg started producing ebooks using ePub formatting. ePub is an open source format standard; most e-readers can read ePub formatting language. "Project Gutenberg offers over 42,000 free ebooks: choose among free ePub books, free Kindle books, download them or read them online" (Project Gutenberg 2013). The goal of Project Gutenberg is to preserve the great collections of the past.

Google Books <http://books.google.com> embraced the concept that the Internet could be used as an index to a vast collection of books. In 2004 the Oxford Bodleian library allowed Google Books to scan some of its rare books. Google reached out to other universities to obtain permission to add the universities' library collections to Google Books. In July of 2007 Google announced, "we [added] a 'View plain text' link to all out-of-copyright books. T. V. Raman explains how this opens the book to adaptive technologies such as screen readers and Braille display, allowing visually impaired users to read these books just as easily as users with sight" (Google n.d.-a). Some of the books scanned for the Google Books project included copyrighted material. Consequently, Google Books is presently in litigation with the Association of American Publishers and the Author's Guild for copyright infringement. The Google digitized collection and current books from various publishers are available for purchase or download through the Google Play online store. A majority of the ebooks in the Google book collection are available in PDF and ePub formats.

World Digital Library <www.wdl.org/en> was created in 2005 by the Library of Congress and United Nations Educational, Scientific and Cultural Organization (UNESCO) with a large donation from Google. "The World Digital Library (WDL) makes available on the Internet, free of charge and in multilingual format, significant primary materials from countries and cultures around the world" (World Digital Library n.d.). This collection includes: maps, drawings, photographs, letters, lithographs, and other ephemera. Also in this collection are many rare and ancient texts, such as *Book of Hours of the Blessed Virgin Mary*, an illuminated manuscript created in the mid-fifteenth century.

HathiTrust <www.hathitrust.org>, a group of research libraries, began digitizing some of their books in 2008. "Launched jointly by the 12-university consortium known as the Committee on Institutional Cooperation (CIC) and the 11 university libraries of the University of California system, the HathiTrust leverages the time-honored commitment to preservation and access to information that university libraries have valued for centuries" (HathiTrust 2008). Presently, the HathiTrust includes over 10,657,589 items from university collections all over the world. A search of the HathiTrust collection will produce a complete ebook unless the item is still under copyright. If the resource is not in public domain, the search findings will list the frequency of certain words and phrases so the researcher can determine if the particular item is a useful resource. The researcher will then be directed to libraries that house the ebook or print copy of the book.

Digital Public Library of America (DPLA) <http://dp.la> opened its virtual doors on April 18, 2013. Initially, DPLA will focus on gathering public domain works from existing digitized collections such as the Public Art Archive and the Smithsonian Institution. DPLA encourages the library community to present digitized resources to add to the collection. Most importantly, "The DPLA will also explore models for digital lending of in-copyright materials" (Digital Public Library of America 2013). Not only will DPLA collect national treasures, but it will work to effect change in government policy concerning copyrighted material. DPLA is a "participatory platform" that encourages public participation in all functions of the library.

Ebook Catalogs

Two large digital catalogs, Open Library and WorldCat, have created catalog entries for many of the ebooks, books, and ephemera published worldwide. Both catalogs list the libraries that house the materials in your area. They publish reviews of their holdings and feature multi-faceted search engines.

Open Library <http://openlibrary.org> is an online catalog of books and a library of ebooks, with the adopted slogan "One Webpage for Every Book" (Open Library 2013). Open Library is the "Wikipedia of card catalogs," and the goal is to list the world's books and ebooks in one catalog. So far, it has over twenty million records from large libraries and individuals who have contributed records that can be added to or edited by anyone. Internet Archive started this wiki project in 2008. Each wiki page includes availability information such as: whether the book can be read (accessed by a hyperlink to the text in the catalog), borrowed, or purchased. Readers can access over one million free ebooks in a variety of formats: ePub, plain text, PDF, and AZW (Kindle formatting language) from the Open Library catalog. The ebooks can be read on NOOKs, Sony Readers, Kobo e-readers, Kindles, tablets and MP3 touch devices (Open Library 2013).

Open Library also links to **WorldCat** <www.worldcat.org>, which advertises the website as "the world's largest library catalog, helping you find library materials online" (OCLC 2013a). Online Computer Library Center (OCLC) began gathering the holdings of university libraries in 1971. "WorldCat connects library users to hundreds of millions of electronic resources, including e-books, licensed databases, online periodicals and collections of digital items" (OCLC 2013b). OCLC developed WorldCat inpart to provide interlibrary loan for books and periodicals. The catalog contains records for more than 23,000 libraries, archives, and museums in over 170 countries that are members of the OCLC network (OCLC 2013c). Ebooks cataloged in WorldCat can be accessed by patrons of the libraries listed in a WorldCat record. To date, there is no mechanism that allows lending of ebooks between libraries. There are some purchasing options such as pay-per-use being developed that may fill this void.

Public Library Ebook Content

Public libraries subscribe or lease ebooks from several ebook vendors including: TumbleBook, Capstone myOn, OverDrive, Axis 360, 3M Cloud Library, GVRL, EBSCOhost, Credo, ProQuest ebrary, and other vendors. If students have public library cards, they can download and read e-titles from the ebook vendors, or download ebooks from the free ebook collections posted on public library websites. School librarians can introduce the students to the public library ebook collection by teaching a library lesson on applying for a public library card. Many public libraries have application forms available on their library website, which can be used to teach the application process. Students would also benefit from a lesson on accessing the public library ebooks.

Patrons at Los Angeles Public Library's seventy-three branches can read ebooks from OverDrive, Axis 360, and EBSCOhost, as well as ebooks from many free sources including Google Books, Project Gutenberg, and HathiTrust. Both Santa Monica and Pasadena Public Libraries subscribe to OverDrive; Pasadena also circulates 3M Cloud Library ebooks. The New York Public Library provides a portal to ebooks from OverDrive, 3M Cloud Library, BookFlix, TumbleBookLibrary, in addition to digitized (Google) books from their own collection. Most U.S. public library city and state systems have digital collections that can be accessed with a public library card's barcode and a pin number.

Santa Monica Public Library (SMPL) system has designated their teen librarian as the liaison to the Santa Monica public schools. This SMPL librarian regularly attends the public school library meetings. Roger Kelly, the youth services coordinator at SMPL, said that the library system has been purchasing additional copies of titles on the schools' reading lists. "We buy lots of additional paperback copies for students to check out, and for the first time last year we also purchased ebook digital copies for the titles that were available, as well, through OverDrive" (2013).

JoAnn Prout, youth collection development librarian in the Omaha Public Library (OPL) system, wrote that OPL's "youth librarians regularly visit local Head Starts, preschools, elementary, middle, and high schools in their area" (2013). Prout also encourages students to request titles through "My Recommendations," a service available on the OverDrive portal at the OPL website.

"MyLibraryNYC is an innovative new pilot program for collaboration between public schools and public libraries in New York City. It encourages student reading by expanding student and teacher access to public library books and removing common barriers to borrowing them" (MyLibraryNYC n.d.). Leanne Ellis the library coordinator for New York City school library services stated that, the MyLibraryNYC collection includes "books, databases, downloadable books, music and movies. New York Public Library (NYPL) has generated a union catalog of all the resources in each participating school." Through MyLibraryNYC students can search all the resources in the New York Public Library and every school library that is a member of MyLibraryNYC. The goal of this project is to create access to all of the school library collections in NYC. "A public library card is all the students need to access the NYC public library ebook collections" (Ellis 2013).

Collaborate with your local public library. Public librarians appreciate teachers' and school librarians' recommendations. School libraries' required reading lists, research project resources, and popular children's or YA titles would be worthwhile additions to the public library ebook collection. In this current technology-driven society students relish access to the latest technological tools such as ebooks, and access to an ebook collection whether at the local library or at a school can enhance students' learning experiences.

□ □ □ ■3

Why Purchase Ebooks?

Advantages of Owning an Ebook

Accessibility

The decision to purchase a book in electronic format rather than print is influenced by numerous factors, not the least of which is access. Being able to review a title at any hour of the day or night is a definite advantage, allowing students to do their research on their own schedules and not be limited only to hours the school library is open. Add to this benefit the fact that many ebooks are available with a license that allows any number of students to access the same title simultaneously, and that one title's reach is greatly extended.

For assignments requiring many students to use the same specific resources, this multiple-user availability may reduce the need for reserve collections of hardcopies with their inherent circulation limitations. We are beginning to see development of some creative approaches to reserve materials; school librarians can sometimes work with vendors to pull together chapters and parts of books and make them digitally available to students as a sort of "course package" on the basis of a per-use fee. This approach is beginning to look more and more practical, and, in time, may prove to be a reliable and inexpensive way to handle reserves.

Ebooks allow a library to extend access to a title in another way as well. Many, if not most, school libraries have chosen to retain their print volumes while building their ebook collections, sometimes duplicating print titles with ebooks. A major advantage to offering access to a title in print as well as digitally is that students with different learning styles can find their own best way to work with the text. In the same way that school librarians might build a collection of audiobooks for those students who are auditory learners, librarians can provide a variety of formats to extend the same options with the printed word.

One California school surveyed reported that students were evenly divided between preferring an e-textbook (49 percent) and a print textbook (51 percent) (Harvard-Westlake 2013). While this preference reflects many variables such as device management, wireless access, and weight of textbooks, it is a clear indication that student preference has not settled on one format or the other at this time.

In providing accommodation to students with learning disabilities, it is important to note that both e-text and print are needed to support this group. The Assistive Technology Training Online Project (ATTO) at the University of Buffalo, addresses the benefits of books available in e-text format, particularly when working with students with learning disabilities. One major difference is that ebooks give students "the ability to change how the text appears. How a student sees the text can impact her ability to read and comprehend. Cluttered pages with little white space and small print makes reading more difficult." It is suggested that students "try resizing the font and controlling the color contrast of the text and background to make onscreen reading easier" (Bauer 2005).

This benefit must be balanced with the ability to control potential distractions that may come with e-text. A substantial number of students surveyed at one school reported that they were worried about their e-readers proving a source of distraction rather than assistance, particularly when a laptop or tablet was used as an e-reader

(Harvard-Westlake 2013). Dedicated e-readers—as distinct from smart e-readers like a laptop, tablet, or smartphone—would tend to reduce this distraction, as access to the Internet and its inherent distractions is limited. This concern expressed by students highlights the fact that students learn best under many different circumstances and that choices must be available to accommodate these differences.

Another aspect of accessibility that should be considered is related to a recent U.S. Department of Justice ruling in *National Federation of the Blind (NFB) v. Philadelphia Free Library*. This decision held that, to provide legally required access for disabled persons, some e-readers must have text-to-speech capabilities and voice-activated controls (NFB 2012). It would make sense for every library that circulates e-readers to have some devices with those capabilities. Currently, the iPad is the most accessible device, but as devices are developed with new features all the time, staying abreast of this issue is important (Minow 2013).

Access to a title can be viewed from yet another angle. The print volume of a history reference book, for example, might have an excellent index and complete table of contents, but the searching capability of a well-developed ebook platform, making use of full-text searching and other powerful search tools, can sometimes shine a light on just the needed passage in a more expeditious way. Add to this one volume a bundle of companion titles in the same field, fully cross-searchable, and students now have a rich and robust wealth of research tools allowing access in a way unmatched by print. The Gale Virtual Reference Library is one example. Searching the term "Flappers" across one library's entire GVRL platform of 61 titles brings in 136 results found in 20 different books. Results are clearly organized by type of publication and type of resource, and are sortable by relevance, document, title, or publication date.

No Shelf Space Required

Another advantage of ebook acquisition is the savings in shelf space—in the case of a title that is not also held in print, that is. If a title is held "in the cloud," the real estate once occupied by that physical volume is released to be reimagined in other, possibly more dynamic, ways.

Durability

Ebooks do not wear out or need to be rebound. They cannot be lost or stolen. In general, with a few notable exceptions that will be explored later, once a title is purchased it is yours until you decide to withdraw it from your catalog. Although many problems remain with ebook management, as we will see, the digital aspect of an ebook remains very attractive.

Changing Technology Affects Acquisition

Importance of Platform

It is impossible to discuss ebooks without an understanding of the technological parameters that support the ebook's acquisition by a library and delivery to the patron. Without the specific technology required for "translation," an ebook is nothing more than disembodied bits adrift in the cloud. As technology is always and inevitably changing, so are the means of acquisition and delivery of ebooks.

In this book we will explore the many ways ebooks are acquired and made available to students. In some cases, changes in ebook delivery will be as simple as the changing names of companies as mergers take place. However, more complex changes can drastically impact the ebook ecosystem, as when a publisher decides not to make its products available at all on a particular system, or when a legal ruling suddenly casts a shadow over a popular circulation practice. One good example is Barnes & Noble's early attempt at ebook management, Fictionwise, which closed up shop in December 2012, leaving customers scrambling to transfer their purchases to another platform. Fictionwise was comprised of several ebook retail websites including Fictionwise.com, eReader.com, and eBookwise.com. As B&N's FAQ explains, "over the past three years there has been a significant decrease in demand for many of the eBook formats that the Fictionwise Websites sold. In contrast, the eBook format supported by B&N, ePub, is growing in popularity" (Fictionwise 2013).

Continuous Improvements

Change is not inevitably bad, however, as we have seen when ebook vendors have taken users' comments and complaints to heart and have worked to improve systems. Originally, OverDrive did not allow patrons to "return" ebooks early, resulting in books' remaining unusable even though patrons had finished them. After much user feedback, OverDrive changed this provision to allow patrons to return ebooks at any time before the due date. This change resulted in a large increase in "circulatability" of the OverDrive collection. In a ripple effect, other vendors are following suit. As the ebook world moves out of its infancy, it is beginning to settle into a more responsible and responsive approach.

Factors to Consider

The decision to purchase an ebook as opposed to a print book depends on many factors, primary among them:

- Is the book available as an ebook that a library can purchase?
- How can students access the ebooks?
- Do students have the choice of reading in print or e-text?
- Is access available from home?
- Is Internet connectivity required to read the material?
- Is the purchasing agreement something the library can manage?

All these questions will be explored in depth in future chapters.

Ebooks and Self-Publishing

Self-published books have long been part of library collections, particularly in the area of local writers and local history. Technology has made it much easier to create one's own ebook, enabling authors who have found it difficult to break into the more rigid world of established publishing to find their own readers. A library curriculum that supports self-publishing would encourage students and faculty to publish ebooks for the school library collections. For those libraries that catalog textbooks, faculty self-published e-textbooks would be added to the textbook collection. Several models are available for self-publishing, with more options entering the market regularly.

Self-Publishing Companies

Amazon (**CreateSpace**), Barnes & Noble (**PubIt!**), and Apple (**iBooks Author**) are among those e-reader providers that have also become established as direct publishers, with varying provisions for bringing authors through the process of making their work available for purchase and bringing the ebooks to the attention of readers. For example, PubIt! (also known as NOOK Press) encourages readers to "Discover Independent Authors."

Other companies facilitating the self-publishing process include **Smashwords, Blurb, Lulu, Outskirts Press,** and **Xlibris**. Each of these self-publishing companies has different features and offers a wide range of services. They will also publish a print version of any book submitted for publication. The pricing for the publication services differs from company to company. Each company lists the various services and prices on their website. Blurb <www.blurb.com> offers Adobe InDesign software for authors who desire to publish ebooks. Lulu <www.lulu.com> converts books presented for publication with an ePub conversion tool. They also sell ebooks on their website. Outskirts Press <www.outskirtspress.com> will convert the book into an iBook edition, NOOK edition or Amazon Kindle Edition ebook. Xlibris <www2.xlibris.com> also sells different self-publishing packages. Xlibris can publish both print and ebook editions or just ebook editions of an author's work.

Smashwords <www.smashwords.com> is a distributor/publisher that publishes ebooks without Digital Rights Management (DRM), which can be a barrier to accessing the ebooks on different e-readers. The Smashwords website states that, "At Smashwords, our authors and publishers have complete control over the sampling, pricing and marketing of their written works. Smashwords is ideal for publishing novels, short fiction, poetry, personal memoirs, monographs, non-fiction, research reports, essays, or other written forms that haven't even been invented yet" (Smashwords 2012). For a subscription of $8.95 a year, anyone can read the ebooks published by Smashwords. Commercial vendors like Amazon and Apple iBooks do purchase books published at Smashwords to sell on their own websites.

Simon & Schuster has even come up with its own self-publishing arm, **Archway Publishing**. Simon & Schuster can supply the design, formatting and marketing services for any books published by Archway Publishing. They offer four different publishing packages: fiction, non-fiction, business, and children's books. The least expensive service package to publish a fiction book using Archway Publishing is $1,999. The elite service package to publish a fiction book is $14,999, which includes deluxe editing, marketing and advertising, among other services specific to this package (Simon & Schuster, Inc. 2013).

This new model for bringing one's work to the marketplace and to libraries has been a boon to authors hoping to make their work more widely available. Increased popularity of self-publishing also benefits libraries who are finding that, as established publishers are frequently reluctant to sell ebooks to libraries, access to these "independent authors" boosts ebook availability.

Self-Publishing Software

There are a few companies that have developed software specifically designed for publishing ebooks, like Apple's iBook Author and Adobe InDesign. Some basic programs can also be used to write an ebook, such as Microsoft Word.

Apple's writing tool **iBook Author** (IBA) <www.apple.com/ibooks-author> uses proprietary formatting but incorporates many of the ePub formatting tools. With iBook Author, enhanced ebooks can be created to include images and embedded video, charts, and other visual aids. IBA is being billed as the perfect e-textbook-publishing tool, but it does not yet offer quite all the tools that e-textbook authors would like. iBook Author is consistently being updated. The ebooks created in iBook Author can be read only on iOS devices (Apple 2012).

Adobe InDesign <www.adobe.com/digitalpublishing/ebook> can be used to design enhanced ebooks in ePub format that can be read on most e-readers. "By supporting open, industry-standard file formats, the Adobe Digital Publishing Solution for eBooks [InDesign] provides an environment in which readers can freely acquire books from a wide variety of sources and read them on a wide variety of devices" (Adobe Systems 2013).

Microsoft Word is an accessible way to create a simple ebook without any enhancements that can then be distilled to PDF format or can be converted to ePub format by self-publishing companies.

E-Textbooks and Self-Publishing

Teachers can publish e-textbooks for students at their local school with publishing software such as iBook Author and Adobe InDesign. These e-textbooks could be added to the school library digital collections. Self-published textbooks can be tailored to the class objectives and district curriculum. E-textbooks can also include videos explaining concepts or interactive quizzes. Some teachers use self-publishing software for publishing individual lessons to supplement the material in commercial textbooks. Other faculty members may choose to create and publish the entire textbook with self-publishing software. One math teacher at The Willows Community School commented that he likes to create some lessons with iBook Author to use in conjunction with the commercial textbook. When students are struggling with the concepts in the textbook, a different approach, provided by the teacher using self-publishing software, can be an effective teaching tool.

The commercial vendors' software CreateSpace, Pubit!, and iBooks Author can also be a conduit for publishing an e-textbook for teacher use at other schools. These unique e-textbooks self-published by the faculty can then be purchased by teachers at other schools who are looking for a different approach to similar material.

Sources of E-Textbooks

For faculty who are either searching for alternatives to the textbooks they are presently using, or who would like to supplement their own e-textbooks with commercial resources, there are a few different options available.

Kno digital textbook company <www.kno.com> has developed an interactive platform that showcases more than 200,000 books from over 80 textbook publishers for K–12 and university classes (Kno 2013a). Some of the platform features include journaling, videos, social sharing, 3D images, flashcards, and quizzes. Instructional videos are imbedded in the textbooks to help clarify difficult concepts (Kno 2013b). Highlights, notes, drawings, or even video from the book can be shared with other students through the social sharing feature. Any diagram students create can be turned into flashcards or quizzes.

E-textbooks are available for rent or purchase at **Barnes & Noble**, **Amazon**, and the **Apple iBookstore**. Barnes & Noble e-textbooks cannot be read on the NOOK, but a downloadable app can be used to read the B&N e-textbooks on a laptop and desktop computer. Many publishers offer ebook versions of their latest textbooks. These e-textbooks can sometimes be less expensive than the print version, but sometimes the "purchase" is actually a license for a single semester's use of the textbook; to use the e-textbook again, another fee must be paid, adding significantly to the price of the e-textbook. Some of the foremost textbook publishers, such as **Houghton Mifflin Harcourt**, **Pearson**, and **McGraw-Hill**, are creating e-textbooks for the elementary and secondary school market.

Barrier to Acquisition of Self-Published Works

As technology defines the method of storage and delivery, however, one author discovered a snag in the system. To make his work available to his local public library, Joe Follansbee, an independent publisher, writer, journalist and blogger based in Seattle, had applied to OverDrive as a publisher. As his work was an historical novel with a local setting, it was a title local public librarians might have wanted to add to their collections. "Seattle Public Library has a strong print collection of local history and local authors, as do most community-based libraries," said Follansbee, who had given print editions of his earlier books to libraries in the past. OverDrive did not accept Follansbee as a publisher, however, and his next step was to offer to give the library the book in ePub and PDF formats, enabling public download. He was told this donation was not possible because it would require distribution via OverDrive. The result, of course, is a classic "Catch-22 situation" (Follansbee 2011).

OverDrive's power to define who is an acceptable publisher gives OverDrive unwarranted power over a library's collection-development choices. Because of DCL's independent development of its own platform, Follansbee would be able to donate a copy of his ebook to the Douglas County Libraries system, but not to his own local library — yet. All the code written for DCL's system is open source, and Jamie LaRue and his team are actively working with other libraries, including school libraries, to help them develop their own systems As LaRue states, "All of our work, including the legal framework and the software we created, is open source and may be freely downloaded and used by any library. Visit <evoke.cvlsites.org> and consider joining us" (LaRue 2013a).

Ebook Devices

Wealth of Options

Ebooks can be read on many different devices ranging from e-readers to desktop computers. Most major ebook vendors now offer ebooks formatted for smartphones, MP3 touch players (including the iPod touch), e-readers, tablets, laptops, and desktop computers. Chapter 2 describes which e-readers and tablets can be used to access the various vendors' ebook collections. If the school librarian has decided to circulate e-readers, the best devices for reading the school ebook collection will depend on which platforms the school is using to access ebooks, the ebook budget, and the school's technology profile. The technology profile might dictate which tablet or e-reader can be used for a library ebook program.

Some schools have adopted a 1 to 1 (1:1) computer program in which every student has a computer or tablet to use. Schools that desire to implement these programs have a wide range of laptops and computer tablets to choose from. In a 1:1 environment ebooks and e-textbooks would be a good addition to the library collection because each student has a device for reading these products. Another school technology program is Bring Your Own Device (BYOD). Students bring in their own laptops, tablets, or other devices for schoolwork. Some BYOD programs stipulate what types of devices students may bring to school. Providing devices for students who do not have access to a device at home is important for a BYOD program to be successful. It is also important to provide e-readers for students who do not have access to devices. Libraries in schools that have not adopted a 1:1 computer program should circulate some devices for students to access vendor and free ebook websites. More information about BYOD and 1:1 programs can be found in chapter 6.

The least-expensive e-readers on the market right now are the basic Kindle and the NOOK Simple Touch. Both of these are dedicated ebook readers. Ebook platforms like 3M Cloud, OverDrive, and Baker & Taylor now download ebooks to the NOOK, Kobo, and Sony e-readers. OverDrive, and Project Gutenberg have an AZW format option for downloading their ebooks to the basic Kindle. Most vendors offer ebooks with ePub or PDF formatting languages that can be read on many devices including the Kindle Fire, but not the basic Kindle because it only reads AZW formatting. More information about vendor formatting languages can be found in chapter 1.

The next tier of devices consists of small tablets like the Kindle Fire, NOOK Tablet, and Nexus 7. These devices easily connect to most ebook collections. They also link to app stores and the Internet. Small tablets can be the best product for schools that want to have computers in the classroom but cannot afford the pricier tablets and laptops.

E-Readers

Importance of Research

Whether a librarian wants to circulate e-readers or wants students to use their own devices to access the library ebook collection, it is important to be familiar with the current e-reader products.

Most e-readers use E ink electronic paper, which looks like a page from a printed book. E ink displays are based on a process that collects tiny particles of ink to create a crisp image. The pigments used in E ink are exactly the same as the ones used in the printing process. Isn't it interesting that the preferred technology for most e-readers mimics the look of the printed page?

Companies that manufacture e-readers are constantly adding new readers to their product lines, and new companies are continually entering the market. One of the more recent additions to the e-reader market is the 3M eReader. In 2011 at ALA Annual Conference 3M exhibited their 3M Cloud library and 3M eReader to the library community. 3M developed the 3M eReader to be synced with the ebooks on the 3M platform (Toor 2011).

The world of e-readers can be a bit mercurial. Pandigital stopped selling their e-readers in July 2012, which is surprising, because the Pandigital e-readers and tablets had only been on the market since 2010 (Alvarez 2012). The lesson to be learned here is that it is important to choose devices from companies that have successfully been selling their product for an extended period of time.

Media recommendations are time-sensitive because the e-reader market is constantly changing and reviews are not always current. Top Ten Reviews does publish a comparison of e-readers every year, and each year the information is updated. Therefore, the reviews are worth reading; see <http://ebook-reader-review.toptenreviews.com>. Good research practices extend to purchasing decisions regarding digital products for the library. Just as school librarians teach students to evaluate resources, librarians need to verify the resources used to evaluate e-readers and find multiple authoritative reviews before deciding which e-reader or other devices will best fit the school library program. Librarians should check with the ebook vendors with whom the school or district has already signed lease agreements to find out which e-readers can read the formatting language for the vendors' ebooks.

Top Ten Reviews has listed the Kindle, NOOK, and Kobo, among the top 9 e-readers reviewed for 2013 (Tech Media Network 2013). The other e-readers reviewed here—the Sony Reader and 3M eReader— also are good basic ereaders. Each of these e-readers have different features and some of the e-readers connect to more ebook collections than others. The Kindle uses a proporietary formatting language and not all vendors' ebooks can be accessed from the basic Kindle.

Kindle Family

The Kindle with a 6-inch black and white screen holds up to 1,100 books, magazines and newspapers, and "free 3G wireless lets you connect"–to the Amazon store of over 1,000,000 ebooks–"from any-where" (Amazon.com 2013a). The basic Kindle and Kindle Paperwhite line read AZW files. Therefore, these readers cannot be used to read the ebooks on many vendors' platforms because most vendors do not offer AZW formatted ebooks. The majority of the ebooks available on vendor platforms are delivered in ePub and PDF formats. Kindle Paperwhite and Kindle Paperwhite 3G are about $60 more than the Kindle. The Paperwhites feature a built-in light and Internet access. The light is projected from the top of the screen and not from behind the text like backlit computer screens on laptops, desktops,

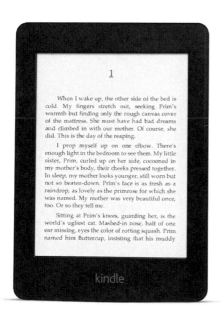

Figure 4. Kindle Paperwhite E-reader.

and tablets. Backlit computer screens can cause eye fatigue, which can be avoided with the Paperwhite lights. OverDrive and Project Gutenberg ebooks can be downloaded to Kindles (Amazon.com 2013a).

NOOKs

Barnes & Noble (B&N) has jumped into the international market, starting with NOOK sales in the UK. Chris Crumm in an article for *Web Pro News* quoted Dean Crammer Head of Category—Computing Hardware, at Currys and PC World. "It's vital, as the UK's leading electrical retailers, that we continually offer the right mix of products… Portable tablet and eReading technology is becoming ever more popular so we are thrilled to be stocking Barnes & Noble's stylish, high quality NOOK products" (Crumm 2012).

B&N plans on expanding product sales to other international markets in the near future. If an e-reader company has a good international base, it is more likely to be fiscally sound. The NOOK Simple Touch and NOOK Simple Touch with GlowLight has a 6-inch black-and-white screen and "hold up to 1,000 books" magazines or newspapers (Barnesandnoble.com 2013b). These basic NOOKs include WiFi for ordering books from the online store, but do not have Internet access. The Simple Touch NOOK reads ebook files in ePub, and PDF format (Barnesandnoble.com 2013b).

Figure 5. NOOK Simple Touch.

Kobo E-Readers

Kobo e-readers with black-and-white display, WiFi, E ink, and simple-turn technology provide access to the "Kobo store of 3,000,000 ebooks" (Kobo n.d. a). All the Kobo products read ePub and PDF formatting.

Kobo Touch, which is just $20 more than the basic Kobo Mini. This e-reader is programmed to read multiple languages. The Kobo website advertises that the Mini is equipped to read "English, French, German, Spanish, Dutch, Japanese, Italian, and Portuguese. Kobo also states, "We're going to be launching more language support shortly" (Kobo, Inc. n.d.-c).

Sony Reader

Sony Reader PRS-T2 is about $40 more than the NOOK, Kindle, and Kobo black-and-white E ink readers. The PRS-T2 has all the same features as the other readers, including ePub support, touch screen, and page turn, and it also offers wireless public library access to OverDrive through the Sony Reader Store. The Sony website states that, "OverDrive, the leading global digital distributor of eBooks to libraries, will now offer visitors to the [Sony] Reader Store an easy way to find collections of eBooks at their local libraries (library card required)" (Sony Electronics 2013).

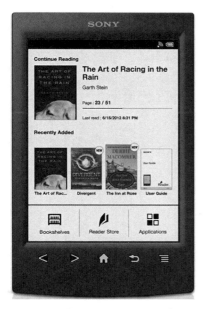

3M eReader

The 3M eReader sells for around $120; so it is the most expensive basic e-reader on the market. It is specifically designed to access the 3M Cloud Library collection. It has a 6" black and white screen, like the NOOK Simple Touch and basic Kindle. Libraries that own 3M eReaders primarily purchased them to access the 3M Cloud Library (3M 2013).

Figure 6. Sony Reader PRS-T2.

Touch Devices and Their Operating Systems

Overview

To access data on tablets, touch technology is used instead of a mouse or keyboard. Most of the leading computer companies have added tablets to their product line in the last couple of years. The most popular tablet at the moment is the iPad. As Erica Ogg mentioned in his May 2013 article on sales figures for tablets in the US, "Apple's tablet sales continue at a rapid clip, increasing every quarter–faster than the iPhone right now…[and] it's still selling more than double the number of tablets each quarter as its closest competitor, Samsung" (Ogg 2013). Other companies also have good-quality tablets that are worth reviewing. Purchasing a tablet just for reading digital products would be a very expensive proposition. However, if a school already has a 1:1 tablet program, the tablets can be used to read the ebooks that are purchased for the school library. Many ebook vendors have added mobile-device access for their platforms.

Mobile products—any handheld wireless device such as tablets, smartphones and MP3 touch players—can connect to the Internet through WiFi or cell phone towers. WiFi is a wireless network access point and is limited to a small area; in contrast, cellular access can create a mobile connection almost anywhere. Some tablets and all smartphones have cellular connections. Three different touch screen mobile operating systems, Android, Windows 8, and iOS, have been developed for tablets, MP3 touch players, and smartphones. The Apple proprietary mobile operating system is iOS; Google's open-source mobile operating system is Android; and the Windows proprietary mobile operating system is Microsoft 8.

Android

Open source systems are not proprietary. Any computer company or individual can use open source technology (Begun 2013). Google purchased Android touch screen mobile technology in 2005, and the first Android phone was released in 2007. Because the software is open source it is free to manufactures that can modify and distribute their own products using Android technology. Over 700,000 applications or apps are available to download to Android devices. Kindle, NOOK, Kobo, and Google Books are just a few of the many e-reader apps available on Android devices (Android n.d.). Most ebook vendors have developed Android apps to connect to their platforms.

The **Nexus 7** tablet, manufactured by Google and ASUS Computer International is an Android device. The Nexus 7 includes a built-in reader that connects to Google Play digital products, which includes over one million ebooks. The Nexus 7 does not have an Amazon or NOOK App, but it can download the ebooks from the Google Play store. Nexus 7 is often compared with the **Kindle Fire** (another Android device) because they are the same size, have many of the same features and are about the same price. The Nexus 7 does have a larger storage capacity than the Kindle Fire and access to more apps. Ebooks in ePub and PDF fromats can be read on the Nexus 7 tablet. Because of the Android OS, the Nexus 7 can be used to access most vendors' platforms (Google n.d.-b).

The **Kobo Arc**, another Android tablet, has a 7-inch screen like the iPad mini. The Arc is quite a bit cheaper than the iPad mini and is preloaded with a few apps that would need to be purchased for the mini. The Arc's basic package (16 GB) sells for around $200. Kobo Arc and Nexus 7 are very similar products. The Kobo Arc reads ePub, PDF, HTML and Plain text formats. Kobo store and Google Books are accessible with the Kobo Arc. The Arc can access most ebook vendors' platforms (Kobo, Inc. n.d.-a).

The **NOOK HD** and **Kindle Fire** are two more 7-inch tablets on the market. Like the Kobo Arc and Nexus 7, they both connect to proprietary bookstores, and have similar storage capacity. The NOOK HD resolution provides a clean, crisp picture. It sells for $199, and can download ebooks formatted as ePub, plain text, PDF, and HTML files (Nook 2013). The Kindle Fire reads plain text, PDF, and KF8 format files, but, because it has an Android operating system, ebooks can be downloaded from Axis 360, OverDrive, and 3M Cloud Library. The Kindle Fire HD 7-inch device also sells for $199, but a 7-inch LCD device is available for $159. The Kindle Fire has an Android operating system (Amazon.com, Inc. 2013c.)

iOS

Apple designed iOS mobile technology for the Apple line of mobile touch screen products. The iPhone, which began production in 2007, was the first Apple mobile touch screen device. The iPod touch, iPad, and Apple TV all use an iOS operating system (Apple Inc. 2013b). iOS mobile technology is a proprietary operating system, not open source like Android. Even though iOS is proprietary and interfaces with the iBookstore, other e-reader apps like Kindle, NOOK, and Kobo are available to download through iTunes; therefore, students and faculty with iOS devices can read Amazon, B&N, and Kobo ebooks. In fact, most ebook vendors have developed an iOS app for their platforms.

Figure 7. iPad mini.

Every year Apple rolls out a new iPad with improved features. The **iPad mini** with a 7-inch screen can be purchased with a WiFi + cellular Internet connection. Now readers can be out of WiFi range and still be connected to the Internet. The iPad Retina display produces high-quality images perfect for viewing picture books and graphic novels (Apple Inc. 2013c). The full size iPad sells for $499, and the iPad mini can be purchased for $329. Apple does offer educational discounts. The iPads have accessibility settings that can be activated for students with visual, learning, physical, motor and hearing disabilities. One accessibility setting "The Voice Over Screen Reader" vocalizes what is on the iPad screen, which is an excellent tool for students with visual disabilities.

Windows

Windows 8 mobile operating system is a proprietary system developed for desktops, laptops, and tablets. Microsoft was working on Windows 8 before Windows 7 was introduced to the public. They wanted to create a mobile operating system with touch technology for the Surface tablets and a line of desktops and laptops (Wikimedia 2013c).

Surface, the new Windows tablet, is similar to the iPad. The applications that are made for the Surface tablet are available at the Windows app store. The Surface tablet uses touch technology, and is equipped with a stylus that can be used to edit documents or record notes with digital ink. Kobo, NOOK, and Kindle apps are available for reading ebooks on the Surface. Microsoft does not have a proprietary e-reader app with a connection to a store that sells ebooks like other devices (Microsoft 2013). The surface RT sells for $499.

Smartphones, iPod/MP3 Touch, and Laptop or Desktop Readers

Smartphones function like a small tablet with cellular connection. All the apps that can be downloaded to read ebooks on tablets will work for reading ebooks on a smartphone. Most ebook vendors have Android and iOS apps, or are planning to introduce their iOS and Android apps within the next year. Readers with iPhones can download the iBook

Figure 8. Surface RT by Microsoft. Used with permission from Microsoft.

app, as well as vendor-specific, NOOK, and Kindle apps. The Android app store has apps for all the popular e-readers and ebook platforms, plus an app for Google Play.

iPods and other MP3 touch devices are perfect for listening to books. If readers don't mind the small screen on MP3 players, they can read ebooks with the same apps offered for smartphones and tablets. PC Magazine lists the iPod touch as the leading MP3 player, "Its better balance of price and performance makes it our Editors' Choice" (Segan, n.d).

Table 5. File formats readable on popular e-readers.

Device	ePub	PDF	MOBI	HTML	AZW or KF8	iBook	Plain Text
Kindle	no	no	yes	yes	yes	no	yes
3M eReader	yes	yes	no	yes	no	no	yes
Sony Reader	yes	yes	yes	yes	no	no	yes
Simple NOOK	yes	yes	no	no	no	no	no
Kobo Mini	yes	yes	no	yes	*no	no	yes
NOOK tablets	yes	yes	no	yes	*yes	no	yes
Kindle Fire**	yes	yes	yes	yes	yes	no	yes
Kobo Arc	yes	yes	yes	yes	*yes	no	yes
Nexus 7	yes	yes	no	no	no	no	no
Surface	yes	yes	no	no	*yes	no	no
Apple iOS	yes	yes	no	yes	*yes	yes	yes
Android	yes	yes	no	yes	*yes	no	yes

* Tablets can read AZW if the Kindle app is loaded.

** The Kindle Fire uses KF8 formatting language to access the Amazon store and is equipped with the android operating system, which can open ebooks published in other formats.

Source: Information from individual e-reader websites and the Wikipedia article "Comparison of E-book Formats" (Wikimedia 2013). Check with the e-reader sales representatives to make sure that the e-readers purchased by a school access the vendor and ebook reader apps used by the school library.

E-Reader Apps

New ebook-product companies are surfacing all the time, offering e-readers, ebook publishing, ebooks, and, now, apps that can be used to read ebooks in multiple formats on many devices that are not dedicated e-readers.

The **Bluefire Reader** app can be used to download any ePub- and PDF-formatted ebooks. Books from most online bookstores and ebook websites can be transferred to an e-reader or other Android or iOS device with the free Bluefire Reader app. Also, ebooks from a mix of different vendors can be downloaded and organized with the Bluefire Reader app (Bluefire Productions 2011).

K-NFB Blio is a free e-reader app that Baker & Taylor has chosen for reading the ePub-formatted ebooks on their platform. Ray Kurzweil worked with the National Federation of the Blind to create Blio. This e-reader app combines Kurzweil's advanced text-to-speech technology with a format that is faithful to the original page layout in print books (K-NFB Reading Technology 2010). Graphic novels, technical journals, and striking coffee-table books are beautifully displayed with Blio. Books checked out from vendor platforms can be loaded on any mobile device or PC, and synced across multiple devices. The Blio store also sells ebooks to read with the Blio app that can be downloaded to Windows, Android and iOS devices.

Adobe Digital Editions is another free reader app that can be used to transfer ebooks in ePub and PDF format from a computer to other devices. Baker & Taylor uses the Adobe Digital Editions software to download ebooks from their platform to NOOKs, Kobo e-readers, Sony Readers and Mac desktops and laptops. OverDrive also downloads ebooks from their platform with Adobe Digital Editons to load ebooks on some devices (Adobe Systems 2013).

If your library purchases or subscribes to an ebook vendor that offers products that can be read on an e-reader or small tablet, it might be worthwhile to invest in a few devices for those students who do not have access to devices at home.

Access for Students with Disabilities

Recently the Free Library of Philadelphia lost a lawsuit because it was circulating e-readers that did not have text-to-speech and voice-activated capabilities (NFB 2012). If a school library wants to circulate e-readers, some of the e-readers should have text-to-speech and voice-activated functions allowing students who are blind, learning-disabled, and physically challenged to navigate the e-reader with voice commands. Also, the ebooks purchased for the e-readers need to have text-to-speech capability.

The iPad does have text-to-speech and voice-activated functions (Minow 2013). To enable the accessibility features on the iPad: Open "Settings," select "General Tools," and then select the features that the school population requires. Different settings are available for vision, hearing, learning, and physical and motor disabilities.

Other ebook companies have expressed interest in creating e-readers with voice-command navigation. Watch the e-reader market

Table 6. Devices circulated by AISL members as reported in AISL Survey 2012.

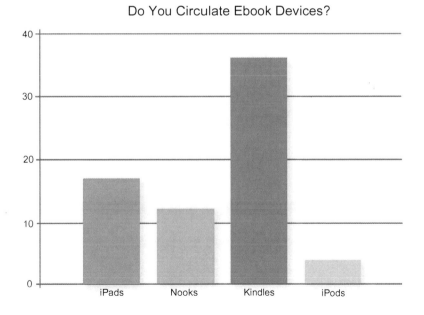

for new products that will accommodate students with physical and learning disabilities. The lawsuit *NFB v. Philadelphia Free Library* and the ramifications for school libraries will be discussed in chapter 14.

All students at a school should have equal access to a device whether the student is physically disabled, learning disabled, or cannot afford an e-reader. The digital divide should be addressed in any school library's acquisition and collection development policy. One of the questions in the AISL survey mentioned in chapter 2 was "Do you circulate devices?" Fifty librarians responded that they do circulate e-readers. Table 6 shows responses regarding circulation and the four devices cited in the survey. In another part of the survey, one librarian mentioned that the school's library was circulating the Kobo e-reader (Leverkus and Acedo 2012). Device circulation and access will be covered in chapter 7.

Device Distribution and Technological Factors

Introduction

Two types of access are available when using library ebooks; students will either download the content to a device, such as an e-reader, laptop, or tablet, or students will read the content directly from "the cloud." With some platforms it is possible to shift between each access type depending on the student's choice.

Online Access

Advantages

Ebooks that are set up to be read online tend to be "device neutral"; that is, the patron doesn't need a specific device or app. Online content can be read from almost any device that allows access to the Internet. These ebooks have the advantage of not being limited to a particular brand of hardware or software. They are most often available either through a library's catalog via URL or through the vendor or publisher's website.

For example, a library might have the digital edition of *Grzimek's Animal Life Encyclopedia* in its catalog, so the ebook is available through the URL in the catalog record. This title is also available through the Gale Virtual Reference Library (GVRL), listed on the library's online resources page. Students might go directly to the ebook if they know what they're looking for specifically, or, if the topic is more complex, they may go to GVRL and do a search across the sixty-one titles that library might own through Gale. Suddenly a single search in one title is multiplied across those sixty-one titles, bringing useful results from titles that might not have been on the students' lists of possible resources.

Online access allows for a useful variety of access points to accommodate a student's needs in different situations. In the case of GVRL, titles can be purchased directly from Gale, either singly or in bundles; the library owns the title and can store the digital files. A small annual fee is charged for hosting the records on Gale's server. Gale is used here as an example, but this is a common model for publishers and vendors hosting their own materials. Other players in this field are ACLS Humanities E-Book, ABC-CLIO eBook Collection, Salem History, and Infobase eBooks.

In the online access category there is a new player. As yet another sign of the rapid developments in the field of ebooks, in March 2013 the vendor OverDrive announced the launch of their new OverDrive Read program. This is yet another hybrid service, in which the vendor supports downloading of titles, but also provides a platform in the cloud, and students can check out books and read them online without having to download them to any device. These options are becoming more widely available throughout the industry. FollettShelf also has options for students to read a book online or as a download. This flexibility will be a key factor in ebooks becoming more fully integrated into the lives and libraries of students and educators.

Challenges

Titles that are so easily read online have a serious drawback, however. They MUST be read online. Often they cannot be downloaded and read later. Connection issues and wireless capability come into play. If a good online connection is not available, the material is not available. The advantage of ebooks that can be downloaded is obvious: Once they have been downloaded, they can then be read offline; connectivity ceases to be an issue.

Downloadable Content

1:1 Schools

The more challenging piece of the access puzzle is device management. For content that is read offline, it must first be downloaded onto some device. This device is generally mobile and could be a laptop, tablet, smartphone, or dedicated e-reader. In a school environment, the first decision will be: Who supplies the device? If the school has a 1:1 program, then most likely each student will have a device, whether provided by the school or by the student as each school's policy dictates. Most 1:1 programs to date involve laptops or tablets, although some schools are investigating a wider range of devices such as smartphones. The advantage of a 1:1 program is the certainty that all students are able to download content onto their devices, as long as the students are set up with the ability to add their own content.

Some schools' 1:1 programs, particularly in lower grades, have built-in limitations about what students can add to their devices. If this type of limitation is in place at a school, additional management will be needed to make sure students are able to get the content they need, whether it is a textbook or recreational reading. If a school allows student downloads, then the 1:1 program is one of the easiest models to manage. This is particularly true if the 1:1 program requires a particular device; if all students have the same device, management can go very smoothly.

A side note on 1:1 programs: Schools can provide the device themselves, at no cost to the student, or as a part of a "lease to own" program. Some schools provide the device to the student for the student's use, with varying limits; the school still owns the device, or the student must return the device at the end of the school year for repair or reconfiguration. When e-textbooks are put into the picture, the device could be considered part of the textbook program. Public schools will likely have systems that are very different from those of private or independent schools.

One element that must be considered when planning for elementary schools is whether students in the lower grades will be allowed to take their devices home. If not, students need print books to take home or access to dedicated e-readers they can check out and take home.

BYOD Schools

Another alternative is to have students provide their own devices in the Bring Your Own Device (BYOD) model. In this scenario the school could designate a particular device, or a particular list of capabilities the student's choice of device must have. For example, a school could specify a laptop, any model that has word processing, Internet connectivity, and a required minimum processor speed and amount of memory. The school-designated device leads to a simpler tech-support scenario, while the student's-choice model will likely require a more robust tech-support environment but could be easier on the students, as they are working with the devices of their choice.

Any talk of required technology brings up the important issue of "the digital divide"; it is true that students and schools with more money have access to more advanced technology, while those with less money have to struggle to keep up. One private school considering entering the 1:1 market did a survey, and found that 86 percent of students said they had their own laptops. There was a good deal of excitement, as one teacher said, "We're practically 1:1 already!" (Leverkus and Acedo 2012). However, further examination revealed that only 52 percent of those students brought their laptops to school regularly. While concern for damage or theft was one reason those laptops stayed at home, students often said that their computers were too old, too slow, not equipped with necessary programs (such as MS Office), or had critically poor battery performance.

It is also important to look beyond the 86 percent of students at that school who had laptops of any type to the 14 percent that did not. Increasing the monetary outlay required for school can be a real hardship for struggling families. This concern must remain at the forefront of any planning for developing an ebook collection, no matter what type of school is involved.

Circulation of Library Devices

For schools that are not 1:1, students who do not have their own devices will need access to them to read downloadable ebooks. The number of devices needed will depend on the amount of e-reading anticipated. When e-reading is limited primarily to recreational reading, having a few devices on hand for circulation might meet the needs of the library's patrons. Devices that are not loaded with ebooks can freely circulate; those loaded with ebooks require a little more care, as described in chapter 14.

The *2012 Ebook Usage in U.S. School (K–12) Libraries* revealed that 25 percent of school libraries offer some sort of device circulation; roughly half of those schools circulating devices allow students to take them home. As expected, the percentage of schools circulating devices increases with the grade level, with 31 percent of public high school libraries and 39 percent of private high school libraries circulating them (School Library Journal 2012).

Most devices circulated by school libraries are some version of the Kindle, the iPad, or the NOOK. Compared with previous years, Kindle and iPad devices have been gaining ground, while NOOK devices have been losing ground. Out of those libraries circulating devices, 74 percent lend devices preloaded with content (School Library Journal 2012). Not only do the devices require management, such as recharging and trouble-shooting, but so do the titles, which must be purchased, downloaded, cleared, etc.

With the proliferation of devices, whether school mandated in a 1:1 or BYOD environment, or student driven acquisition of smart phones, readers and tablets, the subject of charging these devices must be addressed. In the past one major concern when planning new buildings or remodels had been Internet access, so there were often Internet cable ports installed as part of a move toward the 21st century library. These 'wired' connections to the Internet have largely been replaced with wireless models, but the need for access to electricity has only increased. With 1:1 and BYOD programs flourishing, this need must be central in the planning remodel of any new library space or, indeed, in the planning of learning spaces of any kind.

One other issue related to circulating devices with preloaded titles involves legality. As mentioned previously, many publishers of best sellers do not sell their ebooks to libraries, and, if they do, it is at greatly increased prices or limitations in number of circulations per copy. As librarians purchase e-content from these publishers, and load it onto devices that will be circulated, the question arises — is this activity legal? Most "fine print" presented by e-content sellers, and which requires agreement before a buyer can purchase anything, refers to the purchase being for personal and non-transferable use only. When asking Amazon's customer service for clarification, it's hard to get a consistent answer. There has been a general understanding among librarians that it is legal to download one copy of a title to six different devices; if one is able to read the fine print on the legal agreement, it looks like that practice might be legal for a private person, but perhaps not for a library (Leverkus and Acedo 2012).

Since Barnes & Noble and Amazon both have programs through which they sell content to schools, it does seem permissible for libraries to circulate devices with ebooks preloaded, as long as only one copy (per purchase) of any one title is downloaded. Yes, it is a complex point, and one that is hard to pin down. Until this issue is clarified, librarians are wading into murky waters with circulation of multiple copies of a single purchased title. As educators trying to model ethical behavior with respect to plagiarism, copyright, and other legal issues of academia, school librarians need to be clear on this point as well. (See chapter 14 for a more complete discussion of devices and legalities.)

Student-Provided Devices

With student-provided devices, librarians may be spending less time up front, not having to load and circulate devices, but they may spend more on the back end, training students to download materials onto their various devices. For school librarians just starting out with ebooks, a good first step might be to promote e-content available at local public libraries. Presenting workshops on accessing e-content from local public libraries is one way to promote this option. Scheduled for lunch or after school, these sessions can be targeted for students or teachers, and will be welcomed by those who have wanted to access ebooks through the public libraries but hadn't quite started down that road yet. The Free Library of Philadelphia has a useful blog post directed at patrons new to ebooks. It combines clear instructions on the different ebook options available with links to related matter: "Finally, you may discover that not every ebook or audiobook you're interested in is currently available from the Free Library. Find out why here" (Jamie W. 2013). This blog post dated May 7, 2013 is a good starting point for those interested in developing similar guides for their own libraries.

When a school is ready to increase its own e-content offerings, the school librarian and other stakeholders must research and select the right vendor, publisher, and platform for their needs.

Ebook Circulation/Access

Introduction

School libraries that use ebook vendors to supply e-content for their collections provide access to the vendors' products in several different ways. Some libraries have webpages containing lists of hyperlinks to all their different ebook vendors. Others import MARC records for the ebooks into their integrated library system (ILS) with a hyperlink to the vendor platform. Some libraries have a dual system in which they provide both links to vendor platforms through the library's webpage, but also have added MARC records to the ILS with links to vendors' websites. Some school libraries create LibGuides with hyperlinks and usage directions for a school library ebook collection.

LibGuides

Two examples of vendor content access and useage directions are the LIbGuides at Hartford (WI) Union High School and Brentwood School East Campus in Los Angeles, California. Hartford Union High School created a LibGuide <http://libguides.huhs.org/eBooks> for students with search and access instructions that link to ebook vendor websites as well as instructions to access free ebook websites and free ebook publishing sites. The LibGuide also lists instructions for borrowing a Nook. Brentwood school has posted a LibGuide <http://bwscampus.libguides.com/content.php?pid=375550&sid=3076089> with access intructions for the schools' Axis 360, ebrary, and Project Gutenberg ebook collections. The upper school has a 1:1 iPad program. Ebook vendor apps have been loaded on all the iPads so students have access to the ebook collections (Abarbanel 2013).

MARC Records

Jeff Hastings mentioned in a *School Library Journal* article, that for a nominal fee "OverDrive will supply you with MARC records so that your ebooks will show up in your catalog, complete with live links

Figure 9. LibGuide Hartford Union High School

[for] students [to] borrow ebooks directly from your [ILS]" (2011). BookFlix, TumbleBookCloud, Capstone myOn, ACLS-HEB, Axis 360, FollettShelf, MackinVIA, 3M Cloud Library, GVRL, EBSCO ebooks, ProQuest ebrary, Credo, ABC-CLIO and Ingram MyiLibrary also supply MARC records with hyperlinks to the vendor platform. Listing titles in the library's ILS will guide students to ebooks for their research and recreational reading. Some vendors are working with ILS companies to develop ebook circulation software, so that the school's ILS would manage ebook circulation.

Circulation and Access Models

Vendors have developed different circulation and access models for their ebook collections. Four terms will be used to describe the different systems:

- ILS-Managed Circulation/Access—The school library catalog is used to access and circulate ebooks.
- Vendor-Managed Circulation/Access—The student and faculty list is imported to the vendor's site, and circulation and access is managed through the vendor's site.
- Aggregator-Managed Circulation/Access—An aggregator manages all the digital products subscribed to or leased by a school.
- Device Circulation/Access—All of the ebooks are contained on devices, and the school catalogs and circulates the devices and e-content or the school catalogs devices for reading ebooks from the vendors.

ILS-Managed Circulation/Access

The idea that the school library catalog should be used to access and circulate ebooks is popular with many librarians. The ReadersFirst initiative <http://readersfirst.org>, a coalition of librarians working to change ebook lending, invited ebook vendors and ILS companies to a roundtable discussion about electronic lending, held during the ALA 2013 Midwinter Meeting. Michael Kelley, writer for *The Digital Shift* blog, reported on the meeting, "the top distributors of ebooks along with some of their counterparts among ILS vendors [sat] down with leading librarians from the U.S. and Canada…to discuss how the technology and business model for electronic lending should develop" (2013).

This meeting was important because the different vendors have different lending and access models. The librarians, ILS companies, and e-resource vendors that attended this meeting discussed a document drafted by ReadersFirst that listed uniform access requirements for the vendor platforms. If all the different ebook vendors adhere to the dictates of this document, the ebook content would, "be downloadable and manageable in the library's [ILS]" (Kelley 2013).

Baker & Taylor is working with COMPanion Corporation, vendors of Alexandria library software, to create an interface for Axis 360 ebooks to be managed in a school's ILS. According to a COMPanion representative, "this integration option will include the ability for a student to view the checkout status or availability of an eBook from the Alexandria Researcher (browser). Also, it will include the ability to check out eBooks…and to retain checkout information for eBooks. In addition to these abilities, Alexandria will be adding an auto-MARC download directly from Baker & Taylor" (Sauer 2013). SIP2 (Standard Interchange Protocol Version 2.0) software will be used to integrate the vendor and ILS records. SIP2 software was originally developed by 3M to manage check-outs, holds, and renewals through an automated checkout device (3M 2006). Now, with SIP2 software ebooks from a vendor can be circulated through the ILS. The school's ILS can be used to set patron, circulation and item policies for the ebook imported into Alexandria. This full integration process will be available some time in 2014; by the winter of 2013 auto-MARC download and some policy features for ebooks will be available.

Vendor-Managed Circulation/Access

With vendor-managed circulation, ebooks are circulated from the vendor's platform. The librarian or patron sets up an account for the patron's checkout from the vendor. The librarian can usually regulate the checkout period and access. Once the setup has been completed the patron is free to check out ebooks purchased for the specific platform. Vendors typically update the platform periodically by improving the access portal, simplifying the download process, and adding more e-reader options to the site.

Three types of access models are offered by vendors: single-user access, multiple-user access, and unlimited simultaneous access. The type of user access available for a book will determine how many students will have access to the ebook at any one time. Single-user access allows only one student to access an ebook at a time. Multiple-user access will allow a set number of people access to the book.

Unlimited simultaneous access refers to an unlimited number of users that can access an ebook at the same time. GVRL, EBSCO, ProQuest ebrary, and Ingram MyiLibrary lease or offer subscriptions for collections of unlimited simultaneous access ebooks. Follett, Baker & Taylor and OverDrive supply some titles with unlimited simultaneous access, but the majority of the titles available for their platforms are single-user ebooks. Mackin offers unlimited simultaneous access for many of the nonfiction titles available on the VIA platform. TumbleBook, and BookFlix, aimed at elementary school readers, are two ebook subscription services that allow simultaneous access. Information about purchasing single-user, multiuser, and unlimited-simultaneous-access ebooks can be found in chapter 10.

GVRL and EBSCO have added elementary ebook collections to their platforms. All GVRL titles offer unlimited simultaneous access for the ebooks they supply to K–12 libraries. Most of the books available through EBSCO have unlimited simultaneous access, but EBSCO also offers single-access titles and three-user multiple-access titles. These vendors will work with a school library to develop its reference and research collections based on the needs of the school's curriculum. Unlimited simultaneous access is the logical model for ebook research collections when the library budget can support the acquisition of these platforms.

Aggregator-Managed Circulation/Access

Aggregator-managed circulation and access are based on the federated-search model. Any databases, ebooks, and other digital resources that the library leases or subscribes to, can be searched from one plat-form provided by the aggregator. Librarians interested in purchasing the services of these various vendors must make sure that the aggrega-tor supports searching the databases, and ebooks to which the library already subscribes, and that the school's ILS is compatible with the aggregator's platform.

As described on their webpage, "EBSCOhost Integrated Search allows users to simultaneously search EBSCO databases as well as all other electronic resources that they have purchased" (EBSCO Industries 2012). With EBSCOhost, students will potentially be able to search all the library digital resources simultaneously. EBSCO offers another product, EBSCO Discovery Service (EDS), which searches the library's collection of databases, ebooks and other digital resources as well as the library ILS. EBSCO explains that "EDS provides users with access to an institution's entire collection via a single, customizable entry point" (EBSCO Industries n.d.-a). Librarians considering this option should check with EBSCO to make sure that EBSCOhost and EBSCO Discovery Service support the databases and ebooks in the library collection as well as the ILS.

Mackin has developed a limited federated-search platform VIA. The VIA platform can search forty databases and the VIA ebook collection. Mackin will set up ebook bundles to supplement the curriculum or add Common Core State Standards titles and interactive ebooks. Mackin even sells single-user or multiuser bundles, and carries over 37,000 unlimited-user access ebooks. Jeff Hastings, a writer for *The Digital Shift*, mentioned that some of the ebook selections offered by Mackin are subscriptions. "Though most of Mackin's ebooks are yours to share forever, a few publishers, like TumbleBooks and Sesame Street, require annual subscription renewals" (2012).

Device Circulation/Access

Kindles, NOOKs, Sony Readers, Kobo e-readers, and iOS and Android devices owned by a library can be circulated in two different ways. The two circulation options are 1) empty devices circulated for stu-dents to download books from the library ebook collections, and 2) devices already loaded with ebooks. In the interest of digital equality, all students should have access to the school ebook collections. Librarians need to assess the needs of their patrons. Do all patrons have access to a device for reading the library's ebook collection? If they don't, circulating e-readers could be a solution.

Device circulation will add more work to the librarians' schedules because they will need to instruct the students in the use of e-readers and how to download books to the devices. Adobe Digital Editions can be loaded on computers in the library to download ebooks from the school ebook collection to most e-readers with a USB cable. Adobe Digital Edition does limit the number of devices that can download products from one computer. If the library circulates twelve devices, three computers must be used to download books to the e-readers. Both Axis 360 platform and OverDrive do use Adobe Digital Editions to download ebooks to e-readers. Any e-readers with wireless Internet access can download ebooks over the Internet and do not need a USB connection. Librarians will also need to create instruction packets or LibGuides for using any library-owned devices. Some libraries carry a variety of devices for students to use so they can choose the device that will fit their specific needs.

Librarians will have even more work if the library chooses to circulate loaded devices because proprietary e-bookstores do not offer MARC records for their ebooks; therefore, the devices and ebooks will need to be cataloged. Even so, Libraries need to be mindful about paying for each copy of an ebook that they circulate. Mary Minow stated in her webinar "Copyright Licensing and the Law of Ebooks" that libraries should not circulate one title on six different devices. The library should pay for each copy of each title, not purchase one copy of a title and circulate five free copies (2013). More information about circulating loaded devices can be found in chapter 14. Cataloging ebooks is discussed in chapter 11.

Purchase on Demand

A purchase-on-demand (POD) policy would allow students quick access to a particular title. Most ebook vendors add titles to a library's collection on their platforms in a couple of days. Ebooks added to e-readers from an e-reader store will provide instant access to a particular title. The subsequent circulation and students' access to the book is not instantaneous because the library staff must add the items to the ILS so a record for the ebook exists. Once an ebook is added to a particular device all the other ebooks on that device cannot be circulated until the device is returned. Depending on the goals of a specific library's program, the librarian may want to establish an easy way for students to request access to desired ebooks.

Circulation Policy

Any circulation policy will depend on what ebook services the library has to offer.

For Unlimited-Simultaneous-Access Ebooks

An ebook circulation policy for unlimited-simultaneous-access ebooks is not necessary because the books are always available and do not need to be checked in or put on hold. Briefly mention the unlimited access circulation policy, so patrons are not confused.

For Single-User-Access Ebooks

For single-user-access ebooks a circulation policy is needed to specify loan periods, maximum quantity of simultaneous ebooks for each patron, and procedures for holds, renewals, and returns. In addition, students will need instructions for returning ebooks early.

A basic ebook policy would take into consideration each ebook vendor that the library subscribes to or has a license agreement with. Also, a basic circulation policy for school ebook collections should describe each collection, and access and circulation policies.

A basic circulation policy for a collection of e-resources might read:

> **Free eBook Section on the Library Website**: Any of the ebooks in the free ebook section of the library website can be downloaded or read anytime.

GVRL and EBSCO: Students can use any of the GVRL and EBSCO ebooks any time. GVRL and EBSCO ebooks can be accessed through the ILS or the library website.

Axis 360: Axis 360 ebooks are on the library website or can be found by searching the ILS. Up to three ebooks can be checked out for two weeks. After two weeks a book is automatically returned. To continue reading the book it must be renewed. Each book can be renewed for only one more week. Any holds on Axis 360 books will last for only four days after the book becomes available. An e-mail will alert you to the availability of any ebooks you have placed on hold. Check your e-mails and personal Axis 360 site to see if a book you have on hold is available. Your ebooks can be checked in early through the ILS.

FollettShelf: FollettShelf ebooks are on the library website or can be found by searching the ILS. Up to three ebooks can be checked out for two weeks. After two weeks the book is automatically returned. To continue reading the book it must be renewed. Each book can be renewed for only one more week. Any holds on FollettShelf books will last for only four days after the book becomes available. Check your personal FollettShelf site to see if a book you have on hold is available. Your ebooks can be checked in early on the FollettShelf website.

For E-Readers

If the school library circulates e-readers the policy must be more extensive. E-reader policies should include loan periods, fines, procedures for holds and renewals, and policies for damage and loss. The policy needs to define how the e-reader is used. Does the library circulate e-readers with titles preloaded? Or are the e-readers available to access only the library's ebook platforms? Does the school require parents to sign an acceptable use form for the technology on campus? If not, it would be adviseable to create an acceptable use form for the e-readers. It is very important that students and parents understand that they are responsible for loss or damage to the e-readers. Also, students need to know they cannot add content to e-readers.

The Forbes Library in Northampton, Massachusetts, has created a circulation policy for e-readers that stipulates borrowing rules, replacement charges, and circulation policy for most of the e-readers on the market. The library also posts charges for replacing e-reader accessories, cover, stylus, power plug adapter, USB cable, and other hardware that circulates with the devices. To read the policy, go to <www.forbeslibrary.org/policies/e-reader.shtml>.

A basic e-reader policy might read:

> All students in grades 3–12 are required to fill out a technology-use form at the beginning of each year. E-readers can be checked out from the library for two weeks. E-readers must be returned at the circulation desk. If the device is damaged or lost, the price for a new device, plus a replacement fee, will be charged. The replacement fees (in addition to the device's cost) are: NOOK Simple Touch $89, iPod touch $220, and iPad 3 $350. Lost covers cost $25.00, and a lost USB cord or charger is $15.00 each.

Targeting Access for Elementary, Middle School, and High School Students

Librarians acquiring ebooks for elementary, middle school, high school, or school district collections would want to specifically assign appropriate access for ebooks. Some ebook collections such as Book-Flix, StarWalk Kids, TumbleBookCloud Junior, and Capstone Interactive books are geared for emergent readers: elementary school and middle school students. However, most ebook collections are for a broad range of readers. Vendors who supply ebooks for all age groups use different methods for grouping elementary, middle school, and high school collections.

User-Types for FollettShelf

FollettShelf uses patron-type codes to control, which students can check out the different titles. According to Follett, a K–12 school district could create different patron types. For example, a patron type

'Elementary' would be given to every student in the K–5 classes. The same process can be used for middle school and high school students. Once you have finished assigning patron types, then you can designate titles as 'Elementary,' 'Middle School,' and 'High School.' If the designation system is established before the school starts to add ebooks to their Follett digital collection, then the patron designations are easy to maintain. Patron-type terms can also be simply added to an existing FollettShelf collection using a utilities function in the ILS. When an elementary student signs on with their unique user name and password, they will see only the books that have been assigned to their patron-type. The library could also have a designated type for faculty members and, perhaps, parents, which would allow access to all the books in the collection. Only one FollettShelf collection is needed for a school district or a K–8 school because the individual titles can be given appropriate grade-level designations by the school librarians in the district.

Multiple Platforms or ILS Filtering of Access for B&T

Baker & Taylor has two possible solutions for making sure that students access ebooks suitable for their reading ability and maturity: set up multiple platforms for various populations of students according to grade level, or use the ILS to create (and, thereby, filter) student access. A typical school district could have three platforms with age-appropriate ebooks: elementary, middle school, and high school. Of course, according to a B&T representative, the multiple platforms could be set up for any grade structure deemed appropriate for a particular school or district (Bills 2012). Now that Baker & Taylor is working on an ILS-access interface, patron policy in the ILS can specify which students have access to which ebooks. "The integration option that will be ready fall [2013] is patron authentication. This means, a student can log in with their Alexandria user name and password from Axis 360, at which point, Axis 360 will authenticate through Alexandria, checking that the patron is an authorized Alexandria user, and checking your Alexandria patron policies, ensuring that particular patrons can, in fact, check out the ebook" (Sauer 2013). Alexandria is working on a more complete integration option that will include, "the ability for a student to view the checkout status or availability of an ebook from the Alexandria Researcher (browser). Also, it will include the ability to check out ebooks...and to retain checkout information for ebooks. In addition to these abilities, Alexandria will be adding an auto-MARC download directly from Baker & Taylor" (Sauer 2013). Check with your B&T vendor to learn more about this platform ILS access interface.

Authentication for OverDrive

OverDrive uses authentication policies for the different grades. The school librarian will determine which books would be appropriate for which grades. Then, according to a rep for the company, "OverDrive can restrict access to the content each student can see based on their authentication. Example, students in 3rd-grade cannot see material for 5th-grade students, but, if requested, specific students can be given more access (if reading at a higher level or for any other reason)" (Mueller 2013). Individual librarians must decide how practical this method is, given the amount of work required.

Access to All Materials in 3M Cloud

3M Cloud Library lists the ebook collections on their platform by genres and subjects. At the bottom of the webpage ebooks titles are displayed in categories: teen fiction and juvenile (or children's fiction). All the patrons have access to all of the collection.

Other Approaches

The nonfiction vendors GVRL and EBSCO both offer K–12 ebooks that can include reading levels in the ILS record. Other nonfiction vendors Ingram MyiLibrary, ProQuest ebrary, and ACLS-HEB have created ebook collections appropriate for high school and college students. Any of these nonfiction vendors would be happy to set-up a trial to view the ebook collections, which would be a good way to determine what vendor or vendors offer the best ebooks for the school ebook collection.

Developing an Ebook Collection

Introduction

Ebook collection development is similar to book collection development. Some of the key players — aggregators and vendors — offer similar services for both products, but the delivery systems are vastly different. The creation of an appropriate collection-development policy for ebooks requires thinking objectively about the library program and goals, and about special circumstances and interests in the user population. An appropriate collection-development policy will save librarians from spending money on ebook programs that do not suit the needs of the school's faculty or students. Involving other stakeholders is an excellent idea. Showing faculty and students what ebook programs are available and how they can support the curricular goals of the school can result in valuable feedback. Asking the teachers about how they would use ebooks in the classroom and talking to the students about what ebook programs they would like to see at the school can generate useful ideas, as well as buy-in. An ebook collection that has been previewed and accepted by patrons will be in use constantly.

Of course, the availability of digital equipment at a school plays a significant role in the creation of an ebook collection. Do teachers want to project ebooks to share with a class? Does the school have a 1:1 device or BYOD policy, or does the school have a limited number of computers or other devices?

Library program goals will also be an important factor. Is the goal to create a fiction collection of ebooks, or is the focus on acquiring nonfiction or reference ebooks to support Common Core State Standards?

All of these considerations will influence the ebook collection-development policy. (A book about collection development in general and books on many other topics of interest to school librarians are available from AASL; see Appendix B.)

Budget

What is the ebook budget? Ann Behler, information specialist at Pennsylvania State University, wrote an ebook collection-development "Tip Sheet" for ALA's Office for Information Technology Policy Task Force. She stated, "clearly allocate a defined dollar amount to the project. Doing so will keep the project in check and give collections managers a baseline to use when making future decisions" (Behler 2011).

An ebook budget would be based on collection criteria such as whether the library will provide devices or students will provide their own devices, or whether the library will purchase some devices for the students who do not own devices.

Vendor prices will also affect the collection-development budget. Vendor ebook prices vary depending on the number of users, hosting fees, and subscription fees. Will the library be buying one copy of each ebook or an ebook with unlimited simultaneous access? Budgeting will be explored further in chapter 12.

Digital Rights Management (DRM)

Librarians need to be aware of the DRM restrictions on the titles they add to the library ebook collections. Vendors and ebook publishers have used DRM (special codes and mini-software programs in the file for the ebooks) to place restrictions on how libraries purchase, view, and distribute their products. Some publishers might require the library to repurchase an ebook title annually. If the title is not repurchased, the DRM on the publisher's titles will remove the title from the ebook collection. Other publishers restrict ebook purchases to twenty-six checkouts through DRM. These titles will also need to be repurchased after the twenty-sixth circulation. Ebooks purchased through Amazon, Kobo bookstore, or Barnes & Noble are managed through DRM. Eileen Brown discussed DRM rights and ebook stores in her article "Why Amazon is within Its Rights to Remove Access to your Kindle Books" (2012). More information about DRM is in chapter 14.

Choosing Vendors

The type of ebook collection the library would like to develop will determine which vendors are appropriate. Since the available vendors do not all carry the same type of ebooks or use the same kind of platform, many schools use more than one vendor for their ebook acquisitions.

Some vendors concentrate on developing research collections of nonfiction and reference ebooks; examples are MackinVIA, GVRL, ABC-CLIO, ProQuest ebrary, ACLS-HEB, EBSCOhost ebooks, and Ingram MyiLibrary. Their platforms support Boolean search logic to search on titles, authors, publishers, keywords, and, sometimes, full text. Other vendors such as Capstone, TumbleBook, OverDrive, Axis 360, FollettShelf and 3M Cloud Library have focused on developing popular fiction and nonfiction collections, but their search capabilities are not as robust as those of the research-oriented collections. These vendor platforms usually support searching by genres, subjects, authors, titles, formats, languages, and awards.

Reference Collections

School librarians add reference resources to their ebook collections to increase the material available for student research projects and nonfiction reading. Ebook reference collections are easier to search than their print book counterparts because of the robust search capabilities and hyperlinks embedded in the text of e-resources. In contrast, a search of the local ILS for a topic will only provide a list of resource titles. The researcher would then have to check the print books' indexes or open the links to the ebooks to access the titles. A subject search of an ebook reference collection will list which ebooks contain the required information and will also display an annotation that is hyperlinked to the relevant text.

Many vendors offer unlimited-access reference collections that can be customized for a school's curricular needs. Some of the companies that sell database subscriptions are now adding reference ebooks to their packages. Encyclopaedia Britannica and World Book both publish ebooks that are carried by MackinVIA, Follett, GVRL, EBSCO, and other vendors. Britannica and World Book also have their own platform for accessing ebooks. When a librarian contacts local ebook vendors the librarian should describe the school's curriculum and the grades that will be searching the different topics, so vendors' reps can help develop an appropriate ebook reference collection.

Nonfiction

School librarians develop nonfiction ebook collections that supplement and enhance the school curriculum. Nonfiction ebook collections can reinforce and supplement print research resources. The same vendors that have developed good reference print resources — specialty encyclopedias, dictionaries and almanacs — have also developed high-quality e-resources. The same criteria librarians have established to choose print resources apply to development of the ebook collection. The reading level, content, and curriculum needs must be considered for any ebook collections.

Different vendors carry the same ebook titles. For example, the ebook *Animals Up Close* by Igor Siwanowicz is available through Follett, Baker & Taylor, EBSCO, and GVRL. Remember, however, that although Follett and Baker & Taylor have large nonfiction collections, they do not (yet) have the search capabilities of the EBSCO, GVRL, ACLS-HEB, or JSTOR platforms (see figure 10). Examine the collections available through subscription services like ACLS-HEB or JSTOR. They may have the titles students are searching for. School research projects, curriculum, and student interest can all guide nonfiction collection development.

Vendors will set-up free trials so librarians, faculty, and students can assess which vendor will provide the best topics, research tools, and search engine for a particular student body. An elementary school has different research needs than a middle school or high school, and a school district will want to find e-resources for all the schools in the district. Not all vendors carry nonfiction ebooks for all grade levels.

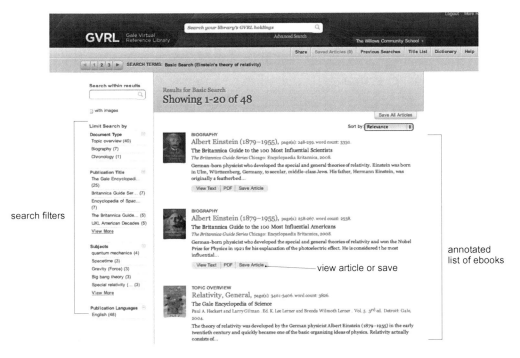

Figure 10. Example of a search for Einstein's theory of relativity in a GVRL collection developed for a K–8 school. From Gale. *Gale Virtual Reference Library*. © Gale, a part of Cengage Learning, Inc. Reproduced by permission. www.cengage.com/permissions.

Fiction

Schools' fiction ebook collections typically contain ebooks for both required and recreational reading. For recreational reading books, one copy of a title is often sufficient, but multiple copies of required reading titles are needed. Most publishers do allow fiction vendors to sell ebooks with the same three access types described earlier: single-user access, multiuser access, or unlimited simultaneous access. The multiple-user ebooks are actually bundles of a set number of ebooks (e.g., twelve copies). Of course, multiple and unlimited access are more expensive than single-user access. Although many nonfiction titles are sold with unlimited simultaneous access at reasonable prices, publishers tend to sell fiction at higher prices, because a majority of their income is based on the sales of popular fiction titles. Some publishers do not sell all their popular fiction ebooks to libraries, due to concerns about financial viability and security.

Publishers are concerned that they will not be able to support the cost of publishing ebooks if they sell their product to libraries for the same price that they charge at ebook stores. Publishers do not charge libraries a higher rate to purchase print books because books wear out and, consequently, have a limited shelf life; in contrast, ebooks can potentially last forever. Some publishers are building in licensing options based on repurchasing or are charging much higher prices to libraries for ebooks.

Alternative Approaches

In July 2011, Douglas County (CO) Libraries (DCL) joined the conversation on ebook availability to libraries with its own ebook manifesto, which clearly describes problems with the relationship between major publishers and libraries, and presents DCL's approach to providing ebooks to DCL patrons. One basic tenet of the DCL business plan is to look for alternatives to the Big Six publishers, and DCL has invested money to support this plan, to the extent of spending $100,000 to build its own local server and design a platform (LaRue 2013a).

Current practice of these major publishers (Hachette Book Group,

MacMillan Publishers, Simon & Schuster, HarperCollins, Penguin Random House)—increasing prices, requiring repurchasing and sometimes limiting title selections of ebooks to libraries—makes independent authors and smaller publishers more attractive. DCL works with small publishers to bring ebooks to DCL patrons (DCL 2012). DCL's director Jamie LaRue suggests librarians should not accept publishers' demands, but rather speak up, as well as find alternate sources of ebooks (LaRue and Hainer 2012). According to LaRue and others, libraries should not be so focused on the latest best sellers but should buy from supportive publishers and "second tier" titles/publishers. Supporting self-published titles is a way to pressure the Big Six. Says LaRue, "In a free market, companies are free to set their prices. But we are free to seek a better deal—and we've found one. Instead of passively accepting what amounts to a 33 percent reduction in the purchasing power of the library, we'll be extending our network of electronic publishers to include those who are more responsive to our needs and budgets" (LaRue 2013b).

In spite of this revolutionary language, LaRue and Gene Hainer (Colorado's state librarian) are, ultimately, hopeful. In the section "Working Together," the manifesto states: "In five years libraries envision a world where they are working together with publishers for the good of all parties; where the ability to publish, find, and buy books is easy, seamless, and sustainable. Ultimately, libraries seek an ebook world without unnecessary constraints on access by and for the public" (LaRue and Hainer 2012).

American Library Association (ALA) and International Federation of Library Associations and Institutions (IFLA) are taking a stand against publishers' pricing policies for ebooks and collection control for libraries. The IFLA e-lending policy paper states, "the implementation of a library's collection development policy has to be in the library's control, and not in the control of publishers and authors" (2013, 3). The good news is that many books that are required reading in middle school and high school are in the public domain and may be available to download for free. A little time spent researching what titles are currently in the public domain can result in saving money for the school.

Ebook Collection Examples

Introduction

Three schools in the Los Angeles, California area—The Willows Community School, Harvard-Westlake Upper School, and Brentwood School, East Campus—have developed different approaches to ebook collection development. The head librarians at each school assessed the needs of the students and faculty, and then they researched the ebook market to determine which ebook collections would match the needs of their communities.

The Willows Community School

Willows Community School (DK–8) acquires ebooks from GVRL, Axis 360, and FollettShelf. The ebooks from these vendors are cataloged in the school's ILS using MARC records, which are hyperlinked to the ebook files for the individual titles. The ebook collections are also posted on the library website with hyperlinks to the vendor platforms. At The Willows Community School, the FollettShelf collection contains elementary research material, curriculum-support material, and picture books for read-aloud. To share information with students or for read-alouds, teachers project the Follett ebooks from their laptops or iOS or Android devices onto interactive whiteboards. They also project picture books so the whole class can easily view the text and illustrations. Since the Axis 360 ebooks can be read on most of e-reading devices the school librarian has chosen to use Axis 360 to develop an elementary and middle school collection of fiction and nonfiction recreational and required reading titles. Axis 360 offers amenities like smooth page turn and narrations for every book.

The Willows Community School has adopted an inquiry-based research program in which students acquire skills in a developmentally appropriate and sequential manner. The lower elementary students search for research resources in FollettShelf. The upper elementary and middle school students search the GVRL reference and nonfiction e-resources to find material for their inquiry-based research projects and presentations. Both GVRL and Axis 360 ebooks are used in the classrooms to supplement instruction and can be projected on the interactive whiteboards. Now that Baker & Taylor and COMPanion Corporation, vendors of Alexandria library software, are developing an ILS interface for Axis 360, access, grade level, and circulation of the ebook collection will be controlled through school's ILS (Leverkus 2013). See chapter 7 for more details about ILS circulation and access.

Harvard-Westlake Upper School

Harvard-Westlake Upper School (HW) in the Los Angeles area uses a variety of vendors to gain access to ebooks. Gale, Salem Press, and ABC-CLIO all supply ebooks that HW selects, title by title, for a one-time purchase price. All of these titles are supplied to the school along with MARC records, so that the ebooks are available both through the school's ILS and by way of each supplier's platform. HW also accesses ACLS Humanities E-Book (ACLS-HEB) on a subscription basis. ACLS puts together a package of 3,500 titles from well-respected publishers, most of which are scholarly publishers or university presses. ACLS provides MARC records for all of their ebooks, so again, the books are searchable through the school's ILS or through the ACLS link on the school's "Online Resources" webpage. As a subscription, the librarian cannot choose the titles one by one, and pays an annual fee to access the collection. These titles are primarily for research projects and curriculum support (Acedo 2013).

Brentwood School, East Campus

Brentwood School, East Campus (high school), circulates ebooks from GVRL, ProQuest ebrary Academic Complete, and Axis 360. The ebooks in the Brentwood GVRL and Axis 360 collections are cataloged in the school's ILS. Brentwood School librarians have created a Lib-Guide <http://bwscampus.libguides.com/ebooks> for their ebooks; one of the pages contains search and access instructions for the Pro-Quest ebrary collection of more than 90,000 titles. GVRL, Axis 360, and ebrary have very useful apps that the librarians have "pushed out" to all the student and faculty iPads in their 1:1 upper school program.

These apps (Gale's AccessMyLibrary School Edition app and Axis 360 Blio e-reader app) are used on campus and at home to download ebooks onto the iPads, so students can read ebooks even when not connected to WiFi. The school librarians also added most of the ebooks from Project Gutenberg to the catalog, with links for downloading.

ProQuest ebrary is proving to be an extremely useful resource for upper school research, especially on projects that are inquiry-based and for which students can choose their own topics. For example, Brentwood owns a few books on Somali pirates, and a handful of students chose that topic for a tenth-grade term paper. The ebrary collection has several books on the topic; therefore, the students don't all have to share the print books. Like the GVRL specialized encyclopedias and ebooks, the ProQuest ebrary books can be used simultaneously by multiple students.

Because of publishers' restrictions for libraries, Axis 360 doesn't always sell the desired titles, and those books they do sell to libraries can cost three or four times as much as the Amazon print price, so that collection is growing slowly. The librarians believe that a high school ebook collection should include the works of John Green and Jay Asher, but the vendor cannot currently supply those authors' works. On the other hand, the 2012 National Book Award winner, *The Round House*, is available through Axis 360. The head librarian has reported that it is really "hit or miss" when trying to purchase titles (Abarbanel 2013).

Collection Development Policies

Topics to Be Covered

A basic collection development policy should include: the library program's objective for ebook collection development, selection criteria, budget, school device and e-reader policies, access model (single, multiple, unlimited), purchase model (lease, subscribe, rent, or repurchase yearly), and weeding criteria.

In general, the objective of school libraries' collection development policies for ebooks is to develop ebook collections that support literacy, curriculum, and research programs, and that accommodate learning disabilities and multiple learning styles. Ebooks provide easy access to research material and titles for required reading. Ebooks can also accommodate the needs of learning-disabled and visually impaired students.

Selection criteria will change with the needs of the student body, the curriculum, and the size of the budget. Free ebooks and ebooks in public domain collections could be used by a school with a limited budget for ebooks. Vendors have prepared ebook collections that support Common Core State Standards. If appropriate, the selection criteria might specify that only Common Core State Standards titles will be purchased.

Sources of Guidance

Many useful resources are available to help create a collection-development policy for digital material. In 2013 Ann Behler wrote the "Ebook Tip Sheets: Collection Development for E-Books" <www.ala.org/offices/sites/ala.org.offices/files/content/oitp/ebook_collection_dev.pdf> for ALA to guide librarians through the ebook collection development process. In 2012 AASL eAcademy presented a new e-course "From 0 to 60: Implement eBooks in Your Library Program in 4 Weeks" <http://www.ala.org/aasl/learning/eacademy/ebooks>. Both AASL and ALA, frequently offer e-courses and webinars about ebook collection development.

Some libraries post collection development policies on their websites. Library colleagues are always willing to share their policies. It would be useful to join a few e-lists and electronic discussion boards where this sort of information is exchanged. See more about peer support in chapter 13.

Weeding—and Disappearing—Ebooks

Ebooks do not need repair or maintenance like print resources, but the weeding process is the same. Amanda Braniff, the librarian at the Montessori School of Denver, described the evaluation process for a print or ebook collection. "The Librarian will continually assess and evaluate the collection. The collection analysis process will take into consideration the age of each item, its continued relevance, and the circulation statistics for that resource" (2010). Ebooks that are not circulating or have outdated content or have been replaced by a new edition will be weeded from the ebook collection.

While librarians need to continually evaluate their ebook collections just as they do their print collections, the ebook format introduces a new wrinkle to the process. Changes in copyright ownership, legal decisions, and new business models can result in titles being erased from a library's collection, at times without notice. With most ebook contracts, the school does not own the ebook; the school has purchased a license to use the digital content, and often that license is clearly stated as "revocable." When copyright issues came to light about George Orwell's novel *1984*, Amazon swiftly — with no warning — removed that title from the device or cloud collection of everyone who had purchased it. (Customers did receive refunds.)

ACLS-HEB notified their customers last year that a number of titles previously available on their subscription service would no longer be available due to copyright issues, and so those records needed to be deleted from customers' ILS databases. Once librarians have begun to accept third-party involvement in collection development decisions when purchasing ebooks by the bundle as opposed to title by title, librarians — including school librarians — need to acknowledge that reality on the other end of the process as well, when vendors tell them which titles patrons can no longer access.

Ongoing Process

An ebook collection development policy should be revised every few years because the ebook publishing world is constantly in flux. Ideally, ebook publishers will soon drop the restrictions they have imposed on libraries, so school librarians can create current collections including popular books students want to read. Meanwhile, checking the current journal articles and blogs about ebooks consistently is a good way to stay informed. (A list of ebook-related blogs is in Appendix A.)

It has been only within the last few months of this writing that HarperCollins has increased the purchase price of ebooks, Random

House has imposed a restricted circulation policy, and Penguin is again selling ebooks to libraries. Publishers' policies will affect development and acquisition policy.

Ebook acquisition is an extension of ebook collection development. Both acquisition and collection development policies need to be structured for the needs of the individual school or school district. Working together, school district librarians or librarians from a consortium of schools might be able to appeal to the vendors or publishers for discount pricing.

Ebook Acquisition

Introduction

The selection and acquisition of ebooks are similar to the selection and acquisition of print books. Many of the same book vendors, bookstores, and publishers that sell books also provide ebooks. Asking favorite vendors about their ebook offerings is a good place to start. So is checking professional journals, such as *School Library Journal* for reviews and articles about ebooks and, most importantly, discussing ebooks with the members of the local library consortium or favorite library online community or blog. Haven't fellow librarians always been the best source for current information?

Vendors

When the ebook collection development policy for the school has been established, librarians are ready to decide which vendors would provide the best resources. The vendors mentioned in chapter 2 are the "big names" in ebooks for libraries at the time of this writing. Vendors will set up free trials of their products. These trials are excellent opportunities to attain input from the faculty and students before signing any contracts.

Acquiring a basic ebook collection for a school might require working with a reference vendor and fiction vendor. A more fully developed collection would require working with more vendors to acquire access to ebook collections that reinforce the curriculum, support research projects, and enhance the fiction section.

Ebook Purchasing/Subscription Models

Proceed with Caution

Vendor purchasing agreements must be read carefully. Hosting fees, subscription fees, access fees, and other costs need to be considered when purchasing a license to access ebooks or subscribing to a vendor service. If anything is not clear in the agreement, vendor reps can clarify the language. More information about licensing ebooks can be found in chapters 2, 10, and 14.

Patron-Driven Acquisition

Some very interesting purchasing models are available from different vendors. One option is patron-driven acquisition (PDA). JSTOR, MyiLibrary, and EBSCO allow students to view titles in the collection, and when one particular title is requested multiple times the library has the option of purchasing that title. The EBSCOhost website describes the PDA process. "Create PDA title lists for your library using specific criteria, and then expose the bibliographic records to [students] without purchasing the titles. A title on the PDA list is triggered for purchase when a patron directly accesses the title, guaranteeing that only those titles with usage are purchased" (EBSCO n.d.-b).

Brain Hive also offers a PDA option. A student can log on to the Brain Hive platform and choose a title to read. The library is charged $1 for the student to access the book. Each time that book is checked out the school is charged another $1. Brain hive keeps track of the circulation statistics for the ebooks. If enough students are interested in a particular title, a purchase option is sometimes available. Some of the publishers that agree to allow Brain Hive to circulate their ebooks are fine with purchasing a long-term license and others will not approve the arrangement (Snell 2013).

Another PDA example is the recommendation feature in OverDrive. As JoAnn Prout a librarian at Omaha Public Library explained, "My Recommendations, an option in OverDrive, allows cardholders to recommend digital titles [for the library to] purchase." By analyzing the titles being requested through "My Recommendations," librarians can determine if more copies of an ebook are needed for the collection.

Short-term Loan

The ProQuest ebrary website states that, "short-term loans provide libraries with all of the benefits of traditional short-term loans with the added advantage of only paying if titles are used." MyiLibrary and EBSCO also offer short-term loans of ebooks to libraries. These vendors can offer titles on the library platform that students can select for their research. The library can decide whether to acquire the title or only subscribe to the title for a brief time. This acquisition model could be a source of e-titles for Inter-library loan. EBSCO will offer long-term acquisition for titles that are consistently requested by the library patrons.

Purchase on Demand Instant Access

Purchase on demand (POD) is an acquisition model that some libraries have adopted to increase patron use and to maximize budget dollars. Patrons help determine the content of the ebook collection using this purchasing model. In one POD model the librarian first purchases ebooks that students and faculty have requested or ebooks that fit the curricular needs of the school. After a basic ebook collection has been formed, ebooks are added through patron demand using the vendors that the school has chosen. Students can request titles that they would like to read on an e-reader and the librarian orders the titles from the vendors. Ebook vendors add titles to their platform within a few days after a library purchases or subscribes to an item. Subsequently, student and faculty requests for ebooks can be filled in a fairly short period of time.

In another POD model, librarians, acting upon student and staff requests, add ebooks to a device through a proprietary store such as Amazon or iBooks. This model, which will require more work on the part of the library staff, is not generally the best acquisition model for ebooks. Under most circumstances, the one or two days required to load an ebook on the vendor platform is not too long to wait for an ebook that can be accessed from the ILS with a MARC record.

Ebook Bundles

Librarians must check the contents of ebook bundles before purchasing a subscription. Does the bundle supply the content needed to support research projects and to supplement the curriculum? Does the bundle contain many titles that would not be used by students? Are the bundles created for the grade levels at the school? The contents of the ProQuest ebrary and ACLS bundles are generally for secondary school collections. EBSCO has developed high school and K–8 ebook bundles; EBSCO also offers subject bundles such as general reference, football, and election-related ebooks. Follett offers starter bundles that can be purchased under a long-term license which can help a library establish an ebook program. Follett also offers subject bundles and grade-level bundles. Credo has developed publisher and subject bundles also available with long-term licenses.

Just as vendors of hardcopy books are also selling ebooks, publishers are publishing titles in both print and ebook formats. Buying ebooks from individual publishers can cost the library more in time and money than buying through an ebook vendor because of the need for additional time to deal with the multiple platforms. Sue Polanka, library blogger (*No Shelf Required*) has written, "… each publisher supplies a unique interface for ebook content. Purchasing from 10 publishers will require libraries to learn, teach, and troubleshoot 10 different interfaces" (Polanka 2013). Many of the titles available directly from publishers can be purchased from ebook vendors with one interface or platform.

Timeframe for "Delivery"

Once an ebook vendor has been chosen and the required licenses have been signed, the ebook collection can be ordered. Vendors typically take two to three days to load the purchased titles to the platform. Batches of MARC records can be downloaded to the ILS fairly quickly.

If the library purchases an ebook bundle, then the collection is available to the students and faculty as soon as the platform has been loaded on the library's website or the titles have been added to the ILS.

Sources of Information

Vendor Reps

Of course, vendor reps are always eager to talk with potential customers. Local consortiums of school librarians can invite ebook vendor representatives from different companies to talk to the group about their products. Viewing the different products in the same room facilitates making informed choices about the best ebook company or companies to support a library program and its goals. Vendor reps will be happy to talk about the current developments for their products. As examples of the dynamic nature of this field, within the last six months Over-Drive has unveiled a new delivery system and platform, and Baker & Taylor added ePub and PDF-formats to their selection of formats so ebooks can now be read on any e-reader except the most basic Kindle. Ebook vendor companies are always introducing new technology for their products. The one way to stay abreast of the latest developments is to stay in touch with the ebook vendor representatives.

Product Reviews

Product reviews are another excellent selection tool. Sign up for e-mail notification or RSS feeds for blogs such as:

> *The Digital Shift: Library Journal, School Library Journal on Libraries and New Media* <www.thedigitalshift.com>

> *Evoke: Creating the Future for Library E-content* <http://evoke. cvlsites.org>

INFOdocket <www.infodocket.com> by Gary Price for *Library Journal*

No Shelf Required <www.libraries.wright.edu/noshelfrequired> moderated by Sue Polanka

PWxyz: The News Blog of Publishers Weekly <http://blogs.publishersweekly.com/blogs/PWxyz>

TeleRead: News & Views on E-Books, Libraries, Publishing and Related Topics <www.teleread.com>

21st Century Library Blog <http://21stcenturylibrary.com> by Steve Matthews

The Unquiet Librarian <http://theunquietlibrarian.wordpress.com> by Buffy Hamilton

ZDNet <www.zdnet.com>

These blogs feature the latest news related to ebooks and compile reviews of the current ebook products. (Additional blogs that also focus on rights to digital content, and on e-reading hardware and software are listed in Appendix A.)

Subscriptions to library journals are crucial in this age of swiftly changing technology. Journals supply commentary on ebook technology, review the latest ebook titles and devices, and publish articles about classroom applications. *School Library Journal, Library Journal, American Libraries, Knowledge Quest,* and *Library Media Connection* are just a few of the journals that publish articles and/or reviews about digital resources and their application in the classroom. Many of the library journals deliver online access to their articles. Some of the journals have both online editions and blogs. One example of a technology-related blog tied to a periodical aimed at librarians is *The Digital Shift* sponsored by the publisher of *Library Journal* and *School Library Journal.*

Webinars

Library publications and organizations also broadcast webinars or online workshops presented by leading authorities on ebooks. For example, useful digital-instruction webinars are available through Learn-ingTimes's Handheld Librarian, *ALA TechSource, AASL eCOLLAB, School Library Journal*, and publishers/vendors ABC-CLIO, Follett, and Library Media Connection. URLs for these and other resources are in Appendix A.

For the past several years *School Library Journal* has produced an online ebook summit featuring seven hours of presentations by noted experts in the digital world. These conferences concentrate on delivering information on the latest ebook technology and library applications. The 2012 conference *Libraries, Ebooks and Beyond* included a panel discussion on tablets in the classroom. (An archived version of the e-conference is still available; see Appendix A.)

In 2012 and 2013 ALA TechSource broadcast several 90-minute webinars that provided pertinent information for the school librarian: "Copyright, Licensing, and the Law of E-Books" by Mary Minow, "No Shelf Required 2: Use and Management of Electronic Books" by Sue Polanka, and "Choosing an eBook Platform(s) for Your K–12 School Library" by Buffy Hamilton. Dan Freeman, online learning manager at ALA, mentioned that the popular webinars are definitely offered more than one time. Freeman commented that since ebooks are a hot topic right now the Minow, Polanka, and Hamilton webinars "will almost definitely be offered again." (Meanwhile, the slides from these presentations are available online; see Appendix A.)

AASL's eCOLLAB: Your eLearning Laboratory is a repository of professional-development resources for AASL members and subscribers to eCOLLAB. Currently two webinars on ebooks are archived at eCOLLAB: "Nooks and eBooks: How They Look in a High School Library" and "Do We Need Books in K–12 School Libraries?" The latter is a discussion about Cushings Academy, a private boarding and day school that removed most of their hardcopy books and purchased e-readers and various ebook subscriptions. New content on a variety of topics is regularly added to eCOLLAB; topics include ebooks, collection development, and multiple literacies.

Acquisition Policy

A written acquisition policy linked to the school library's webpage will explain the selection process, and users with questions about ebook selection can be referred to this policy. An acquisition policy should clearly state selection criteria including who is in charge of selection material, the collaboration with teachers and students, and what materials are acquired.

The following policy of The Willows Community School in Culver City, California, is a sample of a basic acquisition policy.

> The selection of library resources is the responsibility of the librarian. The librarian works closely with classroom teachers and students to ensure that students and faculty have access to a rich and meaningful range of resources that support the objectives of teachers and students, including books, videos, audiotapes, digital audio books, databases, ebooks, and ereaders. Book reviews and other current library literature are consulted, before generating any purchases or subscriptions, to ensure that quality materials are acquired for the library.

A more detailed acquisition policy might list the school's ebook vendors, the types of ebooks sought and acquired, and how much of the library budget will be allocated to acquiring ebooks. The budget might specifically list the allotted amount for each vendor to control balanced expenditures for each ebook collection. Student and teacher ebook requests would help assess the best possible titles to acquire. A complete acquisition policy will help determine whether the library chooses to subscribe, license, rent, or own the ebooks.

One-Time 'Purchase' or Annual Subscription

Introduction

Subscription or purchase? What's the right choice? Some important questions to ask when considering the acquisition of ebooks are: Do I want to own this ebook, or should I subscribe to it for a certain set time? Can the ebook be purchased or is it available only as a subscription? To make an informed decision about subscribing vs. purchasing, some background will be helpful.

Right of First Purchase

Ebooks differ from print books in more than just format. In the United States, copyright issues related to hardcopy books are managed under the First Sale Doctrine, also referred to as the Right of First Purchase. Under this principle, the purchaser of a print book has broad control over what he or she can do with that copy of that book: read it, sell it, lend it, give it away, rebind it. The only restriction on the purchaser of a hardcopy book is that the purchaser can't physically copy it in its entirety; under most circumstances, the protection of the Right of First Purchase extends only to the specific copy that was purchased. The Right of First Purchase does not apply to digital products, including ebooks.

Digital Millennium Copyright Act

Because of the digital nature of an ebook, it is so easy to duplicate that more careful protections were created to preserve the copyright holder's interests. These protections are codified in the Digital Millennium Copyright Act (DMCA), a summary of which is available at <www.copyright.gov/legislation/dmca.pdf>.

Randy Alfred explained in *Wired*, "The new law was crafted to offer copyright protection to authors, composers, filmmakers and other content creators in the new and quickly evolving digital world, both online and off. The problem, as they saw it, was that it was just too easy to make exact replicas of their works. Therefore, the change from paper to digital format requires a different approach to collection development and management" (2008). More information about DMCA can be found in chapter 14.

Licensed, Not Purchased

When a print book is purchased from a publisher or a dealer, such as Amazon, the purchaser owns it outright. When an ebook is "purchased" from a publisher or a dealer, the buyer doesn't actually own it; the buyer has purchased a license to access the digital content. The following restrictions are nearly always stated somewhere in the fine print: "Barnes & Noble.com [for one example] grants the User a limited, nonexclusive, revocable license to access and make personal, noncommercial use (unless User has a business relationship with Barnes & Noble.com) of the contents of the Barnes & Noble.com Site, which includes the Digital Content" (Barnes & Noble 2013b).

In 2009, when copyright issues came to light and it turned out that Amazon did not have the legal right to sell George Orwell's *1984*, Amazon famously applied the "revocable" clause; without

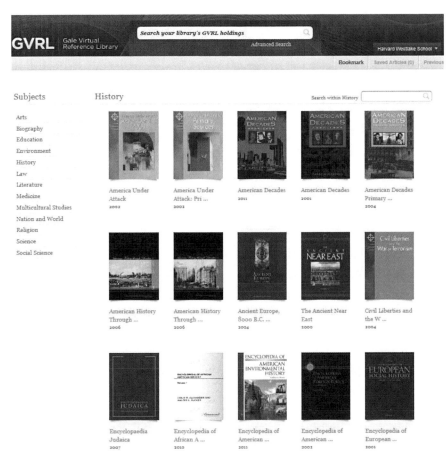

Figure 11. A sample GVRL search result of a high school history collection locates Gale and other publishers' titles. From Gale. *Gale Virtual Reference Library*. © Gale, a part of Cengage Learning, Inc. Reproduced by permission. www.cengage.com/permissions.

notice, several hundred copies of *1984* disappeared overnight from customers' e-readers or clouds. Amazon has since stated that they will give advanced notice in future situations of this type and a refund will be issued. Similarly, under its terms and conditions, Barnes & Noble could conceivably, in rare legal situations, take back (delete) the ebook a library purchased. Other vendors have much the same language in their End User License Agreements (EULA).

Single 'Purchase'

For individuals, the single purchase option is by far the most common type of purchase of a license to use an ebook: one copy of one ebook downloaded onto one device: a dedicated e-reader, a laptop, or a tablet. Often under this single purchase, an individual can make the title conveniently available on four to six different devices, allowing a person to read one book from an iPad, desktop, or phone, as long as these devices are all registered to the same user. The idea is that only the purchaser will use the devices and that the ebook will be "open" on only one device at a time.

However, as mentioned previously, there is some confusion when it comes to a library — as opposed to an individual — making this kind of purchase; in the terms and conditions, the phrase "personal and non-commercial use" becomes critically important.

While the conditions limiting personal use differ from those limiting library use, the single-purchase option is also available to libraries interested in acquiring titles from publishers like Rosen, Infobase, Salem Press, and Gale. With these vendors, a license is purchased once. This license may provide single-user or multiuser simultaneous access, depending on the license and the price.

Gale's platform GVRL (figure 11) allows access to Gale publications as well as other publishers' titles; in this way, GVRL acts in a dual capacity, as both seller and bundler. A single payment is made, and the link to the ebook is delivered, often with cataloging. The link and the catalog record can be added to the library's ILS, and access is activated. When the record comes up in the catalog's search results, a student can go right into the ebook, from home or from school, just by clicking on the URL in the catalog record.

When purchasing access through a platform, it is good to ask whether an annual hosting fee is charged. This type of fee, which is usually nominal, is not uncommon but also not universal. The great majority of titles available through Gale's platform are nonfiction, often reference-type books. Once a library has paid for the title, the only ongoing costs are the hosting fees, if any.

One advantage of providing access through a vendors' platform is that students can often search groups of individually purchased

Figure 12. Sample Salem History search page.

ebooks almost as if they were part of a database. For example, one library might have purchased thirty-five separate ebook titles from Salem Press over the years, and they are all searchable from the Salem Press platform through the school's Online Resources webpage (see figure 12). At the same time, these titles are each available individually, alongside the print version of the book, when a student searches the catalog. Depending on the students' needs, they can simply search the catalog to find individual titles that will be useful, or they can enter the publisher's search page to perform searches across multiple titles in the same arena for a more thorough search.

For this type of purchase, it is important to note that these titles, purchased through vendors and accessed by way of their platforms, are most often provided without an option for download. Sometimes a small number of pages are available for download as a sample, but the content as a whole is only available online. This hosted model is useful as a simple, clean way to access a title without the complication of devices. The down side is that an Internet connection is required to access the book. It is usually not possible to download more than a sample of a title to read offline.

Subscription

The examples explored so far have fallen under the single purchase model. In the case of the subscription model, access to titles is leased every year by paying an annual fee. The titles are always hosted on the vendors' server. The ebooks are not available for download.

As with many rental agreements, it can be to one's advantage to pay a smaller amount to have access to the ebook for a short period of time, with the disadvantage lying in the need to pay year after year. Some examples of this model are ProQuest's ebrary and newly acquired eBook Library (EBL), and ACLS Humanities eBook. These providers are sometimes called "bundlers" as they often select the package of titles that they offer for subscription or, sometimes, purchase.

ProQuest ebrary has developed an ebook platform concept for high schools in which a majority of the titles are acquired through a subscription, a few titles can be added as short-term loans, and other options include a long-term license using either patron-driven access or adding a "perpetual archive" title. Perptual archive is the term ebrary uses to describe the ebooks acquired with their long-term license agreement.

ACLS provides access to nearly 3,700 titles for a very reasonable annual fee, currently $500 per year for a school of 1,500 students. Most of these titles are university presses' publications and similar scholarly editions. Like vendors examined in the single purchase model, ACLS provides both MARC cataloging records and links to the titles, but unlike in the single purchase model, ACLS selects the titles included in the bundle and charges a rental fee annually. In this instance, a library can rent access to an excellent collection of quality nonfiction titles, with the advantage of being able to search individually or among several titles with a single search. Bundlers such as ACLS, ProQuest, and EBL provide the advantages of bundling manageable collections of ebooks on a scale that is often very attractive to smaller libraries, including school libraries.

OverDrive

At the other end of the scale is OverDrive, a well-established ebook management system that got its start in the public library world but which is now actively trying to break into the school library market. Historically, OverDrive has provided large collections of ebooks along with a very user-friendly discovery and delivery service. OverDrive contends that libraries purchase ebook titles from OverDrive, paying only once for each title, and promises that libraries own these titles for as long as they have a business relationship with OverDrive. Half of the fee paid annually by libraries to OverDrive (determined by a sliding scale involving patron numbers among other criteria) goes to administrative costs, while half goes to acquire new titles.

From the vendors' perspective OverDrive is correct in saying that customers have bought the titles. However, if the library wants to make a change, perhaps to adjust to new budgetary restrictions, and does not choose to continue with OverDrive, those ebooks "purchased" over the years will disappear along with the relationship with OverDrive. Because of this reality, OverDrive can be considered in the same category as a subscription. The library must renew the subscription and budget for annual renewals as long as it wants to "own" the ebooks for which it paid in past years.

Jobbers

Moving along the spectrum of access from single purchase and sub-scription models of bundlers, next are jobbers, who sell ebook titles published by a variety of entities. Follett has its platform FollettShelf;

Mackin has Via; Baker & Taylor offers the Axis 360 platform; Ingram has MyiLibrary. These vendors allow the purchase of single titles or whole subject lists, provide platforms with the capability of searching, online reading, *and* downloading for use offline. These are purchases, not subscriptions; these vendors are selling you the license to use their products in perpetuity, with no expiration date, and providing you with a platform to allow management of those products, including circulation control. Via and Follett do not charge annual fees while Baker & Taylor charge a $250 hosting fee for perhaps a smoother interface.

How Will Patrons Access the Resources?

While each of these vendors offers one or more platforms allowing an impressive array of features, the challenge is in pondering how they work together. Is it necessary to select only one of these as a library's primary ebook vendor and manager? If a librarian chooses to go with two or three of them, how do they interact with each other? If they don't interact with each other, how do students find their way along the path to a specific ebook? A public library can be used as an example.

The Los Angeles Public Library offers ebooks through both Axis 360 and OverDrive, with the drawback that these cannot be searched together. The patron must pick one system, search, then go to the other, and search again. At this time, it seems to be a necessary nuisance to search each one in turn, with the possible result that some patrons may give up because of frustration.

Evolving Model

One other element of the single purchase model that builds on some of the advantages of the subscription model is being explored by the pioneers at Douglas County Libraries (DCL), first mentioned in chapter 2. At an average cost of $4 per title, DCL has acquired ten thousand of the top-selling titles from Smashwords, the leading distributor of independently and self-published ebooks. Not only did DCL purchase

| | BOOKS | | | | EBOOKS | | | | |
| | Library Pricing | | Consumer Pricing | | Library Pricing | | Consumer Pricing | | |
Top 10 New York Times Children's Middle Grade	Baker & Taylor (1)	Ingram (2)	Amazon	Barnes & Noble	Overdrive	3M	Bilbary	Amazon	Barnes & Noble
1 Wonder	$8.86	$8.79	$9.81	$10.98	$42.31	$15.99	$8.90	$9.99	$9.99
2 The one and only Ivan	$9.41	$9.34	$10.22	$10.52	$13.99	$13.99	$10.99	$8.99	$8.99
3 The care and keeping of you (for younger girls)	$7.79	$7.66	$8.26	$9.35	*	*	*	$7.85	$9.87
4 Lego Ninjago Character Encyclopedia	$15.00	$10.44	$9.96	$10.79	*	*	*	*	*
5 Out of my mind	$13.42	$9.34	$12.77	$13.02	*	*	$6.99	$5.98	$6.99
6 The care and keeping of you (for older girls)	$7.79	$7.66	$8.26	$9.35	*	*	*	$7.85	$9.87
7 The school for good and evil	$9.41		$12.70	$12.70	$13.99	$13.99	$10.99	$9.68	$10.99
8 Nancy Clancy, super sleuth	$5.53	$5.99	$8.59	$8.99	$4.99	$5.99	$4.99	$4.27	$4.27
9 House of secrets	$9.97	$9.89	$11.25	$11.98	$13.99	$13.99	$10.99	$9.78	$10.99
10 Timmy Failure	$11.84	$8.24	$11.84	$11.83	$14.99	*	$10.68	$9.99	$10.19
Top 10 New York Times Young Adult									
1 The fault in our stars	$9.97	$9.89	$10.24	$10.98	*	$16.79	*	$9.99	$9.99
2 The 5th wave	$10.52	$10.44	$11.45	$11.98	*	$16.79	*	$10.99	$10.99
3 Divergent	$9.97	$9.89	$14.79	$14.94	$7.99	$7.99	$9.99	$5.63	$5.63
4 Insurgent	$9.97	$9.89	$11.44	$11.66	$13.99	$13.99	$12.99	$6.99	$6.99
5 The perks of being a wallflower	$8.40	$8.40	$7.70	$11.20	*	*	$10.20	$7.32	$10.20
6 The rithmatist	$9.97	$9.89	$11.42	$11.42	*	*	*	$8.89	$8.89
7 Looking for Alaska	$10.52	$8.95	$12.83	$13.08	*	$12.59	*	$9.99	$9.99
8 While it lasts	$9.97		$13.34	$13.34	*	*	$9.99	$1.99	$9.99
9 The book thief	$7.79	$7.07	$8.44	$10.98	$12.99	$12.99	$10.17	$9.99	$9.99
10 The elite	$9.97	$9.89	$11.67	$11.90	$13.99	$13.99	$12.99	$10.76	$10.76

6/1/13 issue; source: http://www.nytimes.com/best-sellers-books

* Not available for sale
1 Discounted pricing as advertised on website
2 Actual

Douglas County Libraries is the public library of Douglas County, Colorado, headquartered in Castle Rock, CO. Our annual collection budget (2013) is $3.4 million. We serve a population of just under 300,000. For more information, contact Karen Gargan, Associate Director of Finance, kgargan@dclibraries.org www.DouglasCountyLibraries.org

Figure 13. Douglas County Libraries Report.

these titles outright, rather than just licensing their temporary use, but DCL worked with Smashwords to create a new model of purchase called "library direct," in which authors and publishers determine their own pricing using a web-based pricing tool. This innovation was made possible by the creation and adoption of a very simple tool called the "Statement of Common Understanding for Purchasing Electronic Content," a two-page legal document setting forth in clear language what may and may not be done with the electronic content being sold (DCL 2013c). More information about DCL is in chapter 2 and 8.

Because the authors and publishers at Smashwords are a less traditional group than those over at the Big Six publishing companies, people affiliated with Smashwords seem more inclined to look for creative solutions to the digital stalemate engendered by DMCA and similar legislation. On January 6, 2013 Peter Brantley of the *Publishers Weekly* blog *PWxyz* explored this issue. It is to be hoped that these agreements can be inspirational to those in the more traditional publishing houses, leading them to find similar solutions to make their ebooks more widely available at a more reasonable cost.

Califa, a California consortium of libraries that includes school libraries, has joined with Internet Archive's Open Library and DCL in making commitments to purchase Smashword's most popular ten-thousand titles. Califa provides the opportunity for its members to participate in consortium pricing as supported by Smashwords. In May, 2013, Califa launched Enki Library, a platform that will host and lend library-managed ebooks. Created with open source coding developed by DCL, Enki Library is now available through Contra Costa County Library and San Francisco Public Library, and will soon be serving additional libraries in California, including members of the Bay Area Library and Information System. (Enis 2013).

Fiction Best Sellers

While there are many different ebook providers, and a number of different types of ebooks, it is important to discuss one category of ebooks specifically, as they are in a class apart: fiction best sellers. The great majority of best-selling fiction is published by the Big Six Publishers (MacMillan, HarperCollins, Penguin Random House, Simon & Schuster, and Hachette) who have all put restrictions of one kind or another on selling their titles to libraries. These restrictions have been discussed elsewhere in this book.

While it's not true 100 percent of the time, in the large majority of instances best-selling fiction is available to libraries only as part of one of the large ebook management systems: OverDrive, Axis 360, or 3M Cloud Library. HarperCollins will freely sell a copy of one of their ebooks to a library, with the stipulation that it needs to be re-purchased after twenty-six circulations, albeit at lower rates similar to paperback pricing. Random House will sell their ebooks to libraries, but at three and four times the price they charge individuals. Simon & Schuster and Hachette will not sell directly to libraries under any circumstances, making a partnership with OverDrive or similar provider necessary to gain access to best-selling fiction available in ebook format.

Other more-flexible models are being adopted by larger public and university libraries, although usually with non-fiction titles. These options combine short-term "rentals" with demand-driven acquisition (DDA) and "virtual photocopying" functionality, through which specific chapters and sections of ebooks are made available temporarily for use in course packets and reserves. One version has a library making a title available to students on a temporary basis, and when students use the title a specified number of times, perhaps three, a purchase is triggered automatically in response to the specific profile the library has set up. Ebook Library (EBL), recently purchased by ProQuest, is at the forefront of developing this type of creative, flexible acquisitions model. Librarians can hope that these solutions developed by EBL and others will be supported and, perhaps, advanced with the move to ProQuest.

It is to be hoped that this flexibility might be seen as so successful in the field of scholarly publications that some aspects of it might eventually be adopted by the popular press, particularly with respect to fiction best sellers.

The current state of school library access to best sellers in ebook form is still very limited. June 2013 figures from the Douglas County Libraries Report of ebook pricing show that of the top 10 *New York Times* Children's Middle Grade ebooks and the top 10 *New York Times* Young Adult ebooks, only 13 titles are available to libraries in ebook format, and then only if the library subscribed to both OverDrive and 3M platforms. The most expensive ebook is *Wonder*, priced at $42.31 through OverDrive, although it is available through 3M at $15.99. The print book price for this title ranges from $8.79 to $10.98. It is important to note that the ebook pricing of $7.99 for *Divergent* is the same from both OverDrive and 3M, and that this price is BELOW the print price, which ranges from $9.97 to $14.94 (Douglas County Libraries 2013b).

Of course, many smaller school libraries are not able, or not yet ready, to invest in a system that is as expansive as either 3M or OverDrive. Outside of these vendors, what are the options for accessing fiction ebooks for the school library? The good news is, as of June 2013, Axis 360 provided access to the same titles from the DCL June list that OverDrive did. A brief search for alternatives showed that FollettShelf does not carry any of these titles; this is one area that is changing daily, so be sure to check often. The fact that Axis 360 is now providing library access to so many high-demand fiction titles is very heartening. More companies may join them, providing competition that could lead to greater access and flexibility of platform. In fact, both Axis 360 and FollettShelf do provide a 'start small' option, allowing school libraries to purchase just a few ebooks (with a scattering of 'best seller' titles among them) to begin their collection. These companies allow accounts to be set up with a much smaller initial outlay than OverDrive or 3M Cloud Library.

For the present, however, if a library chooses not to go with the large-scale vendors, one option may be to purchase a title individually and then download it to an ereader for circulation. Ethical concerns discussed earlier lead to the suggestion that this is best managed as one download per purchased title onto one device. While there seems to be increasing access of ebooks to public and larger libraries and a general movement toward more flexible access in these arenas, those trends have yet to make their way into the smaller school library world. It is to be hoped that such limitations will loosen up as publishers and vendors see positive ways of moving forward in the larger library world.

Staying Informed

So many players and models of acquisition crowd the world of ebook management that it is important to gather as much information as possible as librarians move forward with the process of making ebooks available to their patrons. In this area it can be very helpful to join together with colleagues and find strength in numbers.

In one example of homegrown support, the Independent School Library Exchange (ISLE), a consortium of some sixty independent-school librarians from throughout Southern California, joined together to host an Ebook Fair in the spring of 2012. Representatives from ten different ebook publishers and providers each presented the highlights of their programs and answered questions; the presentations were followed by a "mini-exhibit hall," complete with displays and handouts. The experience of being able to hear from different vendors, comparing their programs side by side, while asking questions specific to the needs of one's individual library, was invaluable.

Staying up to the minute with current events in the ebook universe is so important that librarians are well-advised to subscribe to many of the blogs and electronic discussion lists mentioned in Appendix A. Just checking in regularly with these resources will keep librarians abreast of the latest developments in this very volatile field.

Catagloging Ebooks

Purpose

Ebooks must be cataloged for the same reasons print books must be cataloged: to make them easy to find and to keep an accurate inventory of library resources. Many of the same parameters apply to ebook cataloging as to print: find quality records, adapt them to reflect the library's needs, and import them into the library's ILS to allow easy access for students. Up until recently, this advice did not apply to such self-contained systems as OverDrive and 3M Cloud Library, as these records were not generally integrated into the library's ILS. It used to be that, with these systems, the patron had to search for particular ebooks separately from the other resources offered by the library; this is the standard model still in use by most public libraries, in fact. New developments in platform integration, including SIP2 (Standard Interchange Protocol Version 2.0, mentioned earlier in chapter 7), have brought improvements to the way patrons search for ebooks. It is becoming more common to be able to access a vendor's collection of ebooks through the library's ILS in addition to going through the vendor's platform. We're about half-way to a real solution at this time. It is now often possible to search for an ebook through the library's ILS, avoiding the need to separately search the vendor's platform and halting the forced segregation of the collection (go here for print books; go there for ebooks). However, it is still usually necessary, after finding the ebook you want, to then click the link and be sent to the vendor's platform in order to check out the book.However, advancements coming down the pike, including those being developed by Baker & Taylor in partnership with COMPanion Corporation (vendors of Alexandria ILS), are sure to bring even more circulation control back to librarians, possibly as soon as 2014.

Sources of Records

First, where do librarians get the records? Vendors generally supply ebook records through transfer of digital records. Experience has shown that the quality of vendors' cataloging varies widely, so these records must be checked for all the appropriate access points. Librarians who catalog through OCLC may find OCLC's records to be an improvement over those sent by the vendors. The Library Corporation (TLC) <www.tlcdelivers.com> is another source for MARC records as well as other cataloging tools and products.

Maureen Frank, Librarian at Harvard-Westlake Upper School, has found that some vendors provide better cataloging records than others. "What I often do is compare the records for the ebook and those for the hard copy. The hard copy records tend to be very thorough because they are held so much more widely. When I first edited Facts on File records several years ago I found them to be very sparse which is why I went to look at the hard copy record; Facts on File used Sears subject headings and not Library of Congress, which required additional editing. I wanted the e-book records to match the hard copies we already had" (Frank 2013).

However, in the case of large quantities of ebooks entering the system at once, as when a new collection is purchased or a large addition is added to an existing collection (as in the case of ACLS increasing their titles by several hundred at a time), editing of individual ebook records is not practical. (That said, most records will need tweaking as soon as time permits, as described later in the chapter.)

Call Numbers

Librarians will need to decide what to do about call numbers. Some schools use a universal label, for example, "EBOOK," to allow for batch management and easy identification, depending on subject headings and keyword access to enable discovery. As ebooks don't sit on any shelf, location and retrieval are not a reason to assign a particular call number representing a topic.

Subject Headings

For best accessibility, subject headings should be checked to make sure the new ebooks are aligned with the library's system. Many of the vendors use Sears, some Library of Congress; therefore, editing may be needed to suit a specific library. Again, OCLC can be a useful resource, although occasionally ebook records in OCLC do not contain enough subject headings.

Format and Fields to Check

Ideally, each catalog record should be checked for accuracy with regard to format, particularly when adapting a print record into an ebook record. Developing a tip sheet listing particular fields to watch for can be useful.

In particular, the 856 field should be checked. Does the ILS display the =\ [delimiter] z field or the =\ u field? The =\ z field displays text (but is a hot link to the book) and the =\ u field displays the URL. Librarians will want to remove links from the OCLC record and add the link that is the library's access to the ebook in a vendor's cloud or on a vendor's platform.

Another field to check is the 020 field. Extraneous ISBNs in the 020 field must be deleted. This is particularly important as some ILS systems can link records to each other on the basis of a false ISBN "match" if the print ISBN and the ebook ISBN are both included in records. When this happens, the ebook record is in danger of being accepted upon importation as just a copy attached to the record for the print book. The details of libraries' own ILS database formats will differ, but any system that imports records will have criteria on which to judge when to attach a new addition as a copy of an existing record and when to let the new record stand on its own. Taking the time to see what fields are used to match titles in the local ILS will save trouble down the road.

For electronic books, the 245 field gains the =\ h subfield, where _h [electronic resource] is included, identifying the format.

The 300 field ("physical description") requires some attention. You'll see in our sample MARC records that different libraries handle this differently. Record 1 uses the 300 to indicate the original item's physical description, and then includes a 533 to say "electronic resource". Record 3 shows a 300 field indicating "online resource", and then adds a 534 ("original version") note.

The 521 field is especially useful for K-6 or K-8 schools as it includes grade level range and reading level. The 521 0 field in Record 1 below says that this book has a reading level of 5.8 and field 521 1 indicates that the book is geared toward a third to sixth grade reading level.

Cataloging E-Readers Loaded with Ebooks

One method for cataloging devices (NOOKs, Kindles, etc.) loaded with ebooks is to generate catalog records for devices in the ILS and list all the ebooks loaded on the device in the content notes.

Another option would be to create an "equipment" record for each device and catalog each ebook title separately with a note saying which device has the title loaded on it. Each device a library owns will have a unique barcode assigned to it, so when students check out the device, control is maintained.

Yet another cataloging option is to create a catalog record for each ebook loaded on the devices without assigning barcode numbers to the titles. The records of each ebook will refer to the device the title is loaded on. Then the barcode that will be used to check out any ebook on the device is assigned to the device. Students will have an easier time searching for ebooks that have their own catalog record, but this process can be time consuming, particularly if the librarian plans to buy a large number of ebooks for the devices that will be circulated.

None of these options are optimal; they are practical 'fixes' but do not fully address the issue of managing access. Loading multiple titles on devices has another problem built in, however. When any device is checked out for a student to read one title, all the other titles, perhaps as many as fifty or a hundred, are now "unavailable" because they are loaded on the device that is now being used by only one student. This is one unintended consequence of loading many books on one device, and a solution relating to licensing must be found before circulation of loaded e-reading devices can become truly practical.

Sample Records for Ebooks

Here are three different MARC records for three titles in electronic format. These records contain some field information that will be familiar to catalogers everywhere, and some that is unique to ebooks. It is useful to see how vendors and libraries deal with cataloging ebooks in their own ways. While standardization is in some ways the essence of MARC coding, librarians must create a catalog record that meets the needs of their own particular library and patrons, and so we find a variety of approaches to the process.

When reviewing the records below, take special notice of the 020, 245, 300, 5xx, and 856 fields. As you see, some fields are used in the same way from record to record, while other fields are treated differently depending on librarian's specific local requirements.

Record 1. MARC Record for *Golf* by K.C. Kelley.

```
LDR01914pam 2200457 a 4500^
001fol12312217 ^
003ICrIF^
00520080925091202.5^
007cr cnu uuaur^
008080125s2009 miua csb 001 0 eng d^
020 _a1602794111^
035 _a(ICrIF)51939Z^
040 _aICrIF_cICrIF_dICrIF^
05004_aGV968_b.K45 2008a^
08204_222_a796.352^
1001 _aKelley, K. C.^
24510_aGolf_cby K.C. Kelley._h[electronic resource]^
260 _aAnn Arbor, Mich._bCherry Lake Pub_cc2009^
300 _a32 p._bill. (chiefly col.)_c25 cm.^
4901 _a21st century skills innovation library. Innovation in sports^
500 _aTitle proper from title frame.^
504 _aIncludes bibliographical references (p. 31) and index.^
5050 _aHistory of golf -- Developing the rules -- Golf balls -- Golf club technology -- Golf's great
innovators.^
5103 _aWilson's Junior High School, January 2010^
520 _aPresents a brief, illustrated history of the sport of golf, covering the development of the rules, golf
balls and clubs, and the leading innovators in gear and competition.^
5210 _a5.8.^
5211 _a3-6_bFollett Library Resources.^
533 _aElectronic reproduction._bAnn Arbor, Mich. :_cCherry Lake Pub.,_d2009.^
534 _z9781602792623 (trade)^
534 _z1602792623 (trade)^
538 _aMode of access: World Wide Web.^
590 _aeBook^
650 0_aGolf_vJuvenile literature^
650 0_aGolf_vJuvenile literature_xEquipment and supplies^
650 0_aGolfers_vJuvenile literature^
650 1_aGolf^
650 1_aGolf_xEquipment and supplies^
650 1_aGolfers^
653 _aebooks^
830 0_a21st century skills innovation library._pInnovation in sports^
856 _9Alex-
URL_uhttp://www.follettebooks.com/shelf/servlet/Control/1?div=2&cust=0412129&ktsID=68666_3Click
here to read this eBook._yClick here to read this eBook.^
900 _aEbook 796.352 Kel^`
```

Source: MARC record supplied by Follett, edited by librarian using
Alexandria ILS.

Record 2. MARC Record for *Bowling, Beatniks and Bell-Bottoms: Pop Culture of 20th Century America* edited by Sara Pendergast and Tom Pendergast.

```
LDR01711cam 2200349 a 4500^
001gal0787692905^
003MiFhGG^
00520060213174553.0^
006m d ^
007cr un ---uuuua^
008020206s2002 miua sb 001 0 eng ^
020_a787692905 (electronic book)
020_a9780787692902 (electronic book)
040 _aDLC_cDLC_dMiFhGG^
24500_aBowling, beatniks, and bell-bottoms_h[electronic resource]_bpop culture of 20th-century
America._cSara Pendergast and Tom Pendergast, editors.^
260 _aDetroit, Mich._bUXL_cc2002^
4901 _aGale virtual reference library^
504 _aIncludes bibliographical references and indexes.^
5051 _av. 1. 1900s and 1910s -- v. 2. 1920s and 1930s -- v. 3. 1940s-1950s -- v. 4 1960s and 1970s -- v. 5
1980s and 1990s.^
520 _aRecounts the enduring products, innovative trends, and fun fads of the past ten decades. In 5
volumes.^
533 _aElectronic reproduction._bFarmington Hills, Mi:_cGale,_d2002._nAvailable via World Wide
Web._9Farmington Hills, Mi:^
534 _pOriginal:_e5 v. : ill. ; 25 cm.^
650 0_aPopular culture_zUnited States_xHistory_y20th century_xMiscellanea_vJuvenile literature^
651 0_aUnited States_xCivilization_y20th century_xMiscellanea_vJuvenile literature^
653 _aebooks^
7001 _aPendergast, Sara.^
7001 _aPendergast, Tom.^
7102 _a Gale Group.^
830 0_aGale virtual reference library^
856_uhttp://galenet.galegroup.com/servlet/eBooks?ste=22&docNum=CX3425199999_9Alex-URL_3
Available via Gale Virtual Reference Library. Click here to access_yAvailable via Gale Virtual Reference
Library. Click here to access^
900 _aebook 306.09 Bow^`
```

Source: MARC record supplied by Gale, a part of Cengage Learning, and edited by librarian using Alexandria ILS.

From Gale. *Gale Virtual Reference Library.* © Gale, a part of Cengage Learning, Inc. Reproduced by permission. www.cengage.com/permissions.

Record 3. Sample of Harvard-Westlake Upper School OCLC MARC record for *American History Through Literature, 1820-1870.*

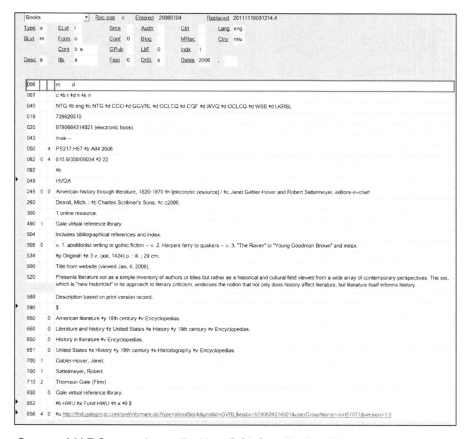

Source: MARC record supplied by OCLC, edited by librarian using Destiny ILS.

Work with the library's cataloging utility to make sure all the proper fields for an electronic book are included. Other sources of help in finding out more about the ebook cataloging process are available. One example is the Cataloging and Metadata Services page on the Pennsylvania State University Libraries website: <www.libraries.psu.edu/psul/cataloging/catref/eresources/ebookscataloging.html>. The ILS vendor's customer support staff will also be able to assist librarians in getting started with cataloging ebooks.

Cataloging is as much an art as a science, so there is room for differences in the MARC records of resources from one library to another. However, the bottom line for any cataloger is access. Can students find the title easily? Is the information that is provided clear and unambiguous? Are any local requirements (reading levels, special collections, curriculum links) built in to the record as needed? While ebooks are a new format, these basic guiding principles are timeless.

Budgetary Factors

Introduction

In many ways, budgeting and paying for ebooks are much the same as for print titles. The ebooks that are purchased under the single purchase model are paid for once, just as a hardcopy book is, though nominal ongoing hosting fees may apply. Ebooks that are acquired under the subscription model parallel subscriptions to periodicals that must be renewed each year. As libraries become more dependent on periodical databases and the number of print magazine subscriptions declines, these two formats become even more similar.

Familiar Paradigm Shifts

In the past, librarians carefully selected their magazines and journals title by title; then periodical databases came along and became increasingly more sophisticated to the point that, using ProQuest as an example, a librarian has no say in what particular titles are included in a ProQuest subscription (which is "bundled") and, perhaps more importantly, the librarian has no say in how long ProQuest keeps the digital content. Add to this the issue of "rolling walls" (when a publisher has an agreement with ProQuest that the past three years, for example, will not be available online to protect the publisher's stream of revenue) and occasional holes in coverage due to copyright issues, and the periodical database becomes more and more like the ebook world every day.

This example illustrates that today's librarians are already accustomed to bundled inventory and annual subscriptions. The idea that when a librarian drops ProQuest students have no further access to those titles is not a surprising one. In this way, the subscription model for ebook acquisition is not new at all. In fact, in some ways it's even easier to budget for subscriptions to ebooks than for print books or singly purchased ebooks, as the subscription fees are much the same year after year, with adjustments made for gradual increases to match inflation.

Reconfiguring budgetary line-items to reflect the realities of ebook expenditures may be needed, just as any change in the library program requires adjustments. Just as when items previously listed as "Magazines" turned into "Periodical Databases," reexamining spending patterns will be needed after getting into ebook purchases and subscriptions. Allocations for these, like any other expenditures, must be reassessed annually. Line-items might break down into different subdivisions than before. Priorities change, and percentages allocated to specific line-items also change. After working with ebooks for awhile, librarians may find that the structure of the budget for the library program would benefit from reorganization.

Potential Problems

Librarians must watch out for rough waters ahead, though. When Penguin dropped out of OverDrive, all those titles that librarians had "purchased" through OverDrive may still be available but suddenly all other Penguin titles become unavailable. Titles that may be available today for "purchase" by libraries through systems such as Over-

Drive may not be available in the future, depending on contractual changes.

As Penguin, one of the Big Six publishers, has some very desirable titles in their catalog, this lack of availability certainly cuts into OverDrive's ability to sell itself. Indeed, given the peculiar constraints of the OverDrive contract, by which a library has access to "purchased" books only as long as the library remains an OverDrive customer, budgetary decisions must be reexamined in a new light. If a librarian becomes unhappy with OverDrive's product due to the fact that one or more major publishers have dropped out of its service, does the librarian have the flexibility to change vendors?

While some budget-related factors are entirely predictable, some changes on the horizon are not yet developed fully enough for librarians to predict effects on budgets. The innovative models of EBL, such as demand-driven acquisition and rent-to-own options could lead to useful new paradigms in the field of ebook acquisition. Librarians will need to keep a weather eye out for developments on the horizon. Keeping informed by reading blogs, such as those listed in Appendix A, will help keep librarians up to date.

13

Librarian Support Groups— Learning From Peers

The American Library Association (ALA) provides professional development and lobbies for the interests of the membership. ALA president Maureen Sullivan (2012–2013) has been diligently meeting with publishers and asking for realistic ebook pricing and availability of popular titles. ALA Washington staff members are focusing on lobbying congress for changes in the laws that govern library use of ebooks and collection development.

An important focus of ALA is providing professional development opportunities to the membership community. The American Association of School Librarians (AASL) and ALA have produced webinars, conferences, and e-conferences to educate their membership. Also, ALA and its divisions use journals, blogs, and e-lists to communicate with the librarians the organization serves. State and national library organizations also provide professional development opportunities through conferences and consortium meetings.

School Library E-Lists and Online Discussion Boards

Many school library organizations around the U.S. and internationally have developed e-lists and online discussion boards (also known as listservs) for their members. These resources furnish librarians with a large community of peers with similar interests, concerns, and goals, and e-list queries can stimulate a multitude of useful answers. Having access to a large group of librarians to discuss new technology, answer any curriculum, literacy, and learning-skills questions, or disseminate information provides an excellent support system.

Many state library associations also have e-lists. Librarians can contact their state associations to find out how to register to participate in online discussions. Below is a selected list of national and international school library e-lists. The e-mail discussion lists below are for association members only, with the exception of LM_NET, which is open to any school librarians that subscribe to the list.

AASL Forum — American Association of School Librarians <www.ala.org/aasl/about/community/lists/forum>

AASL ISS — Independent School Librarians section within AASL <www.ala.org/aasl/aboutaasl/aaslcommunity/aaslsections/iss/resources>

AISL — Association of Independent School Librarians <www.aislnews.org>

IASL-LINK — International Association of School Librarianship <www.iasl-online.org/about/handbook/iasl-link.html>

ALA INFOLIT — K–12, public, and academic library discussion list for information literacy <www.ala.org/aasl/about/community/lists/infolit>

LM_NET — "Where School Librarians Connect" <http://lmnet.wordpress.com/subscribe>

School librarians interested in adding ebooks to their libraries' resources can ask members of electronic discussion lists what they are doing to develop ebook collections and what they have read about ebooks recently. Reading all the current articles about ebooks is a daunting task, but if a personal learning community of friends send out bulletins about the latest ebook news, members can acquire valuable information to make informed choices about ebook services. Staying in touch with other librarians in your area is beneficial for many reasons, including staying aware of ebook collections other librarians have developed and the articles they have read. Members of an e-list will definitely open e-mail with the subject line "Did you see the article about...?"

Regional Consortiums

Valuable Resource and Possibility of Saving Money

Librarians at independent schools, or schools that are not part of a large school district should consider joining (or organizing!) a local library consortium. An example of a consortium of smaller school distrincts is the Genesee Valley Educational Partnership. Christopher Harris wrote an article about the creative funding and financial advantage for members of the Genesee Valley Partnership. He mentioned that the consortium can arrange group pricing and "pool money from individual libraries to leverage group purchasing" (Harris 2013b). The Southern California Independent School Library Exchange (ISLE) and Bay Area Independent School Librarians (BAISL) organizations work on finding the best pricing on vendor products for their members. One approach that they found to be successful was to invite vendors to their meetings.

A group of elementary and middle school librarians that would like to meet the ebook vendors in their area might invite Capstone, TumbleBooks, BookFlix, Follett, Baker & Taylor, Gale, EBSCO, and Britannica to come and present their products. Any group of librarians, whether they are from a school district, a consortium of schools districts or an assembly of independent school librarians, can benefit from viewing different ebook platforms and discussing the ebook products of various vendors.

ISLE's Event

ISLE, a consortium of more than seventy-one middle school and high school librarians in Southern California, invited ten different ebook vendors and publishers to exhibit their products. Each presenter was allowed five minutes to speak to the group. During the five-minute presentations, the presenters displayed their ebook platforms, performed searches, and demonstrated ebook functionality. After the presentations, the ISLE members were given the opportunity to visit with the individual vendors at booths arranged with computers to access the vendors' websites for sampling the digital products. All of the vendors offered discounts on hosting fees or ebook bundles as well as special promotional prizes. A few lucky schools won a free subscription for one year to ABC-CLIO database/ebooks. Gale Cengage created a sale package for ISLE members who wanted to purchase GVRL ebooks. Gale also offered to replace the libraries' Gale print titles with digital titles from the GVRL collection at a discounted price.

When the librarians finished perusing the vendor booths, they sat down together to review the various vendors and their products. The consortium members discussed the ebook platforms that were presented and asked each other questions about the platforms that members were currently using. It was important to hear why each librarian had selected specific vendors for the e-content in the school. The presentations and discussions helped many of the members choose ebook platforms that would match the needs of their specific faculty and student body.

The ten ebook vendors and publishers that presented their products were: MackinVIA, OverDrive, Baker & Taylor, Follett, Credo, Infobase, Rosen, ABC-CLIO, GALE, and EBSCO. Britannica sent brochures but Britannica's ebook representative was unable to attend the meeting. Oxford Press reps. were also unable to come. ProQuest would have been another good vendor to invite; some of the ISLE members subscribe to the ProQuest ebrary Academic bundle.

BAISL's Event

BAISL, a San Francisco Bay Area library consortium of over one hundred elementary, middle school, and high school librarians, held an ebook fair. Because BAISL is a large group of librarians with mixed grade levels, more vendors were invited to their ebook meeting than the Los Angeles meeting for middle school and high school librarians. Many of BAISL's members are working with the vendors they met at the meeting, which was an excellent opportunity to find the right vendors to help the librarians develop ebook programs for their schools.

Local Ebook Professional Development, Peer Mentoring

The Southern California Chapter of the California Association of Independent School (CAIS) organized a professional-development seminar on school ebook collections. Organizers invited the authors of this book to come and speak to a group of librarians about basic elementary, middle school and high school ebook collection development, purchasing models, and legal and ethical concerns. Librarians attending the conference ranged from ebook neophytes to those more familiar with ebook collections. The presenters discussed the different vendors' products, and during the discussion the more-savvy ebook users described their ebook collections' assets and issues.

School librarians' peers are one of the most valuable resources available when librarians are faced with making decisions about any library products.

Surveys

Survey data on ebook usage, vendors, devices, and ethical practices, gathered from the members of a state or national library association, can also be useful. As mentioned in chapter 5, in 2012, 105 librarians from the U.S. and Canada who are members of AISL (Association of Independent School Librarians) filled out a survey that was prepared by the authors of this book. Most of the librarians who responded to the survey had ebook collections and many of them expressed a desire to enlarge their existing collections.

The response to the question "How long have you leased, owned, or subscribed to ebooks?" ranged from fifteen years to less than a year. Out of the 96 responses to this question, a majority of schools have added ebooks within the last three years.

In answer to the question, "Are you satisfied with the ebook product?" 62 participants answered "yes"; 28 responded "somewhat"; and only 4 participants answered with a straight "no." The very satisfied customers were using nonfiction ebook collections like GVRL, ProQuest ebrary, and ACLS-HEB. The most common reasons that the members answered "somewhat" were: ebooks for libraries are expensive, the platforms are not easy to use, vendors cannot supply ebook versions of many of the popular books, devices loaded with ebooks are difficult to maintain and catalog, or the subscription collections did not contain enough titles to support the school curriculum. These were the same reasons mentioned by school librarians who answered "no" to the question. A majority of the people who answered that they were not satisfied with their ebook collection had worked with only one vendor to acquire ebooks for their schools. The school librarians that were satisfied with their ebook collections were working with multiple vendors.

School District Ebook Collections

Introduction

Many school districts are creating useful ebook collections for their members. Some school districts are providing devices for students through 1:1 or BYOD programs that offer students access to district-wide ebook collections. Looking at the local school districts' ebook program can provide valuable information about creation and implementation of ebook programs. Checking out the websites for nearby school districts is a good idea, as is contacting the local school district to ask if they are thinking about designing any ebook programs. School district librarians who are knowledgeable about ebook vendors and programs can even suggest which ebook vendors might be the best match for a school district.

Below are brief descriptions of ways a sampling of school districts have made ebooks and other e-resources available to their students.

Los Angeles Unified School District (LAUSD)

On June 19, 2013 Apple announced that it had reached an agreement with LAUSD to supply iPads for all the schools in the school district. "Education is in Apple's DNA and we're thrilled to work with Los Angeles Unified public schools on this major initiative as they plan to roll out iPads to every student across 47 campuses this fall," said Philip Schiller, Apple's senior vice president of Worldwide Marketing" (Apple Inc. 2013a). In 2014 the rest of the schools in LAUSD will distribute iPads to their students. If all the Los Angeles school district schools provide tablets for their students, each student will have an ebook reader to access the ebook platforms available to students in the district. LAUSD has developed a "Digital Library" portal to a large selection of digital products <http://notebook.lausd.net/portal/page?_pageid=33,551496&_dad=ptl> including EBSCO, Salem Press, and Project Gutenberg ebook sites.

New York City Department of Education

Through the MyLibraryNYC program the New York Department of Education worked with public libraries to develop a union catalog of the resources available in many of the NYC public schools so the schools can share resources and also access the large ebook collections available to students through the public libraries in the city. More information about MyLibraryNYC is in chapter 2. Information about the program is available online at <http://nycdoe.libguides.com/MyLibraryNYC> and at <http://mylibrarynyc.org/about>.

Hillsborough County Public Schools

Hillsborough County (FL) Public Schools (HCPS) have instituted a district-wide ebook program for students. The ebook vendors and publishers that the district schools work with to develop their ebook collections are: myON Capstone Interactive Library, Axis 360, GVRL, Britannica, ABC-CLIO, Salem, and Infobase. All the digital resources are accessible through a portal on the school district's website <http://lms.mysdhc.org>. The school district also has a hyperlink to the state and county public library ebook and database collections. The Florida Electronic Library does not require a library card to access the electronic resources, but the Hillsborough Public Library does require a library card to access the e-content.

Kansas City Public Schools

Kansas City Kansas Public Schools (KCKPS) have an online portal <http://schoolweb.kckpl.org/INDEX.html> for access to the e-resources, including TumbleBooks and Gale ebooks. Pages for elementary, middle, and high school students also link to the Kansas City Kansas Public Library (KCKPL) and Kansas State Library e-resources <www.kslib.info/digitalbooks/3m.html>.

The KCKPS page for high school students directly connects to the database page at KCKPL. This is an excellent example of public library and school district digital cooperation.

Other Examples

Small school districts throughout the U.S. have also started ebook programs for their students. In suburban Denver, Cherry Creek School District subscribes to ebooks through OverDrive and ABC-CLIO. A professional development collection of ebooks for the faculty and staff has also been acquired. The ebook collection of Cherry Creek School District can be searched in the SyrsiDynix ILS <www.cherrycreekschools.org/DLVMS/Pages/default.aspx>. An ILS for the whole school district will allow the students to find resources at all the schools in the district.

A group of small school districts can band together to create a consortium with more financial clout for negotiating with vendors. The Genesee Valley Educational Partnership in northeastern New York used Mackin as an aggregator to develop a collection of ebooks for the twenty-two small school districts in the area. "The goal was twofold: pool money from individual libraries to leverage group purchasing, and increase the efficient use of existing funding" (Harris 2013b).

In another article by Harris, he describes the collaboration of Genesee Valley Eductional Partnership, Mackin, and *School Library Journal* to create a new ebook selection website, "Here Be Fiction." The new website offers "school library-friendly licensing terms, with titles readily available for licensing by school libraries for both individual and multi-user access" (Harris 2013 a). The e-titles can be accessed through the MackinVIA platform. More information about this website can found in chapters 2 and 15.

Legal and Ethical Considerations

Introduction

School librarians perform five main roles: program administrator, teacher, information specialist, instructional partner, and leader (AASL 2009, 16–18). In the capacity of teachers, librarians guide their patrons to legal and ethical practices such as citing the work of others, observing copyright restrictions, and upholding ethical standards. Becoming well informed about the latest laws and acts affecting library practices can be a daunting task because laws change to accommodate new technology and people work to change laws that are not effective or practical.

ALA and AASL work hard to influence positive change in copyright and intellectual freedom laws, to protect the rights of librarians and library users, and, most importantly, to keep the membership informed and educated about changes to the law through publications, webinars, and conferences. Copyright law is not static but is in flux, particularly now, in part because ALA is working to correct some of the problems related to implementation of the Digital Millennium Copyright Act (DMCA), which was the most recent major change to copyright law.

The Copyright Act of 1909 was revised in 1976. "Congress noted that extensive technological advances had occurred since the adoption of the 1909 Act. Television, motion pictures, sound recordings, and radio were cited as examples. The Act was designed in part to address intellectual property questions raised by these new forms of communication" (Wikimedia Foundation. 2013b). Twenty-two years later in 1998, the DMCA was enacted in answer to concerns that copyright laws created in 1976 did not adequately cover the needs of companies, individuals creating digital products, and their users. The Internet and computers were in their infancy in 1976. That year Steve Wozniak and Steve Jobs were building computers in a garage, and Jimmy Carter and Walter Mondale were exchanging e-mails about the upcoming campaign. The next year, Radio Shack and Commodore had also entered the Personal Computer market. In 1979 Jobs and Wozniak introduced Lisa, the first personal computer with a graphical user interface (Zimmermann 2012). In 1998 — when President Clinton signed the DMCA — Microsoft was a prominent company in the computer industry, Google had opened its first office, and the American public was embracing e-commerce (Google Inc. n.d.-c).

Members of congress believed that the new copyright regulations were necessary to protect the rights of digital inventors. The intent of DMCA was to establish copyright laws for digital content and to stop Internet piracy of digital products. Digital Rights Management (DRM) is one of the copyright controls that the DMCA copyright law protects.

Digital Rights Management

Anne Behler described DRM in her 2011 "E-book Tip Sheet" for collection development. DRM refers to access technologies that are intended to limit how the general public uses digital resources. DRM is used by digital content vendors, digital publishers, hardware manufacturers, and digital copyright holders to restrict how ebooks can be viewed and what purchasers can do with them.

The Electronic Frontier Foundation (EFF) combines the expertise of lawyers, policy analysts, activists, and technology professionals to educate and advocate for the general public. On the Foundation's website ramifications of DRM are discussed. Did you "[buy] an ebook from Amazon but can't read it on your ebook reader of choice? That's DRM" (EFF n.d.). Vendors of ebooks use DRM to limit viewing ebooks to specific platforms, and ebook publishers have placed restrictions on how libraries purchase, view, and distribute publishers' products. A publisher's purchase policy may require libraries to repurchase titles each year. The built-in yearly expiration date (enforced by special codes in the ebook files) is an example of DRM. Every library's collection policy should account for the DRM policy of the vendors or publishers the library uses to license, purchase, or subscribe to ebooks.

Digital Millennium Copyright Act

The American Library Association has developed a webpage <www. ala.org/advocacy/copyright/dmca> that defines DMCA and its impact on copyright. The page also provides links to other valuable resources about DMCA.) Excerpts from that webpage and others will enhance an understanding of DMCA.

"On October 12, 1998, Congress passed the Digital Millennium Copyright Act" (ALA 2013b). The law became a part of the Copyright Act in 2000. The World Intellectual Properties Organization (WIPO) met in 1996 to discuss digital rights and the Internet. "The DMCA was designed primarily to sufficiently address the…WIPO treaties signed at the Geneva conference during December of 1996" (Worchester Polytechnic Institute 2010).

"Despite the work of libraries and other partners dedicated to preserving the traditional balance in copyright law between protecting information and affording access to it, the DMCA tilts strongly in favor of copyright holders" (ALA 2013b).

A brief explanation of a few notable sections and titles of the DMCA will illuminate the impact of this law on libraries.

Section 1201 "imposes rules prohibiting the circumvention of technological protection measures" (ALA 2013b).

It is illegal to remove the DRM from any ebook so it can be read on another device. DRM-removal software is readily available, but it cannot be used legally. However, sometimes people remove DRM to back up the ebook in case the company that published the ebook disappears. Section 1201 does not change Fair Use Law, which is discussed below.

> Title II. "sets limitations on copyright infringement liability for online service providers " (ALA 2013b).

The online service provider, which can be a library that is providing online services for students, is not liable for user copyright infringement caused by a student transmission from the institution. The library is required to remove any copyrighted material that is saved on library computers if the copyright owner requests the removal, but library staff members are not required to search for materials until notified by the copyright holder.

> Section 404 "provides a significant updating of the rules and procedures regarding archival preservation" found in Section 108 of the Copyright Act. (ALA 2013b).

Three copies of a digital work owned by an institution can be made to preserve the work. Most libraries license — not own — copies of ebooks. Libraries that license digital work cannot copy the entire content of an ebook, but libraries that own a digital work can make three back-up copies.

> Section 403 "mandates a study of distance education activities in networked environments" (ALA 2013b).

In response to input from constituents, members of congress asked the Copyright Office to study the needs of distance learning, specifically educational broadcasting for online courses, because the original wording in DMCA was very restrictive. Congress passed The Technology, Education and Copyright Harmonization (TEACH) Act in 2002. The TEACH Act allows online courses to display books, magazine articles, graphics, paintings, videos, music, plays, etc. within the parameters of Fair Use (Worchester Polytechnic Institute 2010). This is just one example of how libraries and other institutions work to press for revisions of DMCA so that it reflects the needs of the user as well as the author and publisher.

Section 104 "mandates a study of the effects of anti-circumvention protection rules on the 'first sale' doctrine" (ALA 2013b).

Through the dictates of First Sale Doctrine in the 1976 copyright law (also referred to as the Right of First Purchase) the owner of a hardcopy book could circulate the book, give the book to a friend, loan the book to another institution through Inter-Library Loan, or sell the book. A digital book is not a physical copy of something and cannot easily be shared in the same manner as a print book, and ebooks are usually acquired through a license agreement, not owned, so the library cannot sell something it does not own. The DMCA task force felt that First Sale Doctrine as it applies to digital works should be set aside for further study. Recently, First Sale has resurfaced as a subject of discussion in the media. It will be interesting to see how First Sale will be applied to ebooks in the future. See chapter 10 for information on First Sale.

Fair Use

Section 107 of the copyright law includes a list of the reasons for which creating a copy of a specific item may be considered fair. According to the U.S. Copyright Office, "Fair Use" applies to using copies of material "for criticism, comment, news reporting, teaching, scholarship, and research" (2012).

The definition of Fair Use is deliberately ambiguous so that a broad interpretation can be made of the four principles that will apply to any conceivable situation. The four principles used to determine if Fair Use applies to the particular use of a copyrighted material are:

1. The purpose and character of the use, including whether such use is of commercial nature or is for nonprofit educational purposes

2. The nature of the copyrighted work

3. The amount and substantiality of the portion used in relation to the copyrighted work as a whole

4. The effect of the use upon the potential market for, or value of, the copyrighted work (U.S. Copyright Office 2012)

These principles apply to ebooks as well as other digital resources. The TEACH Act has applied the principles of Fair Use to digital resources effectively. Now, teachers can broadcast parts of books, magazine articles, videos, music, plays, etc. The TEACH Act can be applied to physical or digital copies of a work. The amount of each item used is limited to a portion of the entire work.

If using a large portion of a copyrighted resource, it is best to somehow transform it or to contact the copyright holder and ask for permission to ensure compliance with the copyright law. Some ebook vendors, such as GVRL, EBSCO, and ProQuest ebrary, allow educators to download portions of the ebook. Other vendors do not allow portions of their books to be copied, but under Fair Use it might be fine to make a screenshot of a portion of a book—educators must remember, though, to apply the four questions to any use of a copyrighted work.

One example of fair use doctrine applied by the judicial system is the ruling in the case *Authors Guild v. HathiTrust*. The court found that HathiTrust did not break any copyright laws. The ruling stated that the HathiTrust's creation of digital copies of works in university libraries would be covered under Fair Use. Some of the wording in the final-judgment document was, "I cannot imagine a definition of fair use that would not encompass the transformative uses made by Defendants' MDP [Mass Digitization Project] and would require that I terminate this invaluable contribution to the progress of science and cultivation of the arts that at the same time effectuates the ideals espoused by the ADA [Americans With Disabilities Act]" (HathiTrust 2012).

This ruling refers to the ADA Act because HathiTrust resources are accessible for the visually impaired. The Authors Guild has filed for an appeal of the judge's ruling. Members of the Guild view the HathiTrust collection as a collection for all people not just the visually impaired. Fair Use usually applies to a part of a book but under the ADA Act a book can be copied in its entirety to accommodate disabled access to the material. The HathiTrust collection is also mentioned in chapter 2.

For more information about Fair Use, librarians can read the books *Copyright for Schools*, 5th ed. by Carol Simpson (Linworth 2010) and

Complete Copyright for K–12 Librarians and Educators by Carrie Russell (ALA 2012). Both explain copyright law as it applies to educational use of copyrighted material.

Device Accessibility

Mary Minow presented a webinar "Copyright, Licensing and the Law of E-Books" in February 2013. She discussed current lawsuits that have recently been settled. Minow warns librarians to be cautious about purchasing e-readers for circulation and to make sure that some of the e-readers fit within the parameters of the Department of Justice access ruling in *NFB v. Philadelphia Free Library*. The National Federation of the Blind (NFB) sued Philadelphia Free Library because it was circulating e-readers that were not accessible for visually impaired individuals.

In the Department of Justice decision for the case *NFB v. Philadelphia Free Library*, the court cited two existing laws: the Americans with Disabilities Act Title II and section 504 of the Rehabilitation Act of 1973 to support its findings. This decision supports the fundamental concepts of federal disability discrimination law, namely: "the obligation to provide an equal opportunity to individuals with disabilities to participate in, and receive the benefits of, the educational program, and the obligation to provide accommodations or modifications when necessary to ensure equal treatment" (U.S. Dept. of Ed. 2011). The court required the library to buy ten new fully accessible devices as accommodation to the blind patrons at the library and within four years the library will be required to circulate only fully accessible devices (NFB 2012).

"Fully accessible" means the e-reader must have text-to-speech capabilities and voice-activated controls. Simple NOOKs and the most basic Kindle are not fully accessible e-readers. Libraries circulating only those devices should add some accessible e-readers to the collection. The iPad is one of the most accessible devices on the market right now. After this ruling, many other e-reader companies will probably add disability-support features to their devices as well. Researching devices, including availability of text-to-speech and voice-control features, before purchasing them is important. In her webinar, Sue Polanka mentioned a couple of particularly useful sites. One that provides comparisons of features important for serving patrons with disabilities is Diagram Center, which is managed by Benetech, a nonprofit organization dedicated to innovative technology solutions to solve social problems. The comparison chart is available at <http://diagramcenter.org/research/product-matrices-complete.html#eb_hardware>. Another useful website she mentioned is that of Reading Rights Coalition <http://readingrights.org>; the Coalition's site includes links to organizations that are members of the group. Those organizations' sites include information about serving people with various disabilities, including visual and motor impairments.

Device Circulation

To provide services to students who may not have e-reader devices of their own, libraries are circulating e-readers in a number of different ways. It is Mary Minow's opinion that unloaded devices and their software can be circulated under the principles of First Sale Doctrine because the e-reader is a physical object. First Sale Doctrine, as previously mentioned, allows the owner of a book, movie, music CD, e-reader, computer, or other physical object to give away, resell, or lend that item to anyone (Minow 2013).

One Copy of an Ebook for Each Device

In her webinar Sue Polanka addressed the issues encountered in the process of lending e-readers. Both Sue Polanka and Mary Minow discussed the option offered by most e-reader companies of downloading one title to six different devices, and they agreed that this model is for an individual user not a library. They recommend that libraries purchase every copy of an ebook circulated in their collections (with the exception, of course, of free ebooks). Erin Crumm, vice president, corporate communications at HarperCollins, has stated, "We allow a purchaser to access an ebook on up to six different devices simultaneously, since many readers switch from one device to another during the course of the day. If we were to extend these terms to libraries, a library could circulate six copies of an ebook in perpetuity based on a single purchase." If a library purchases one copy of a printed book, the library has only one copy to circulate. Circulating one book on six devices would mean that a library was circulating one purchased copy and five free copies.

In Mary Minow's opinion, the best way to circulate e-readers is to circulate unloaded devices so patrons without their own e-readers can download and read ebooks in the library's collection. The next best use of an e-reader by a library, in Sue Polanka's opinion, is to circulate "copyright free books from Project Gutenberg, or other distributors of public-domain books, or creative commons license or any other unrestricted content" (2013).

Polanka mentions that Amazon and Barnes & Noble have both developed management tools that administer the downloading of ebooks for a collection of e-readers. These companies obviousy do not object to schools using their ebooks; Amazon and Barnes & Noble market their management tools to schools and businesses with multiple devices. Whispercast at Amazon and Barnes & Noble's download service for multiple e-readers place one copy of a title on each e-reader. Both Sue Polanka and Mary Minow stated that this is not the preferred way of circulating ebooks in the library. The cataloging of the content of e-readers is much more complicated than cataloging vendor ebooks.

Concerns about Leasing Ebooks from Commercial Stores

Commercial stores such as Barnes & Noble, Amazon, Kobo Books, and iBooks all have lease agreements that limit the rights of the purchaser. Amazon removed copies of George Orwell's *1984* and *Animal Farm* from their patrons' Kindles because of copyright restrictions. (Customers did receive refunds.) Brad Stone, a columnist for the *New York Times* contacted Amazon to find out why they removed the ebooks. He stated in his article, "An Amazon spokesman, Drew Herdener, said in an e-mail message that the books were added to the Kindle store by a company that did not have rights to them... 'When we were notified of this by the rights holder, we removed the illegal copies from our systems and from customers' devices, and refunded customers'" (2009).

Amazon and Barnes & Noble have both removed accounts for some of their customers in the last year. The vendors were within their rights to remove these accounts because users must accept the license agreement before they are allowed to access the screen used to create an account. The Amazon license agreement states, "All content included in or made available through any Amazon Service, such as text, graphics, logos, button icons, images, audio clips, digital downloads, and data compilations is the property of Amazon or its content suppliers and protected by United States and international copyright laws" (Amazon. com 2013b). Eileen Brown, in an article on the blog *ZDNet,* wrote about Amazon summarily deleting the accounts (and all purchased books therein) of customers who—it turned out—did not actually have any problems with their accounts. It was an error on Amazon's part, but one that resulted in a judgment and punishment without the benefit of a defense (Brown 2012).

Barnes & Noble and the iTunes Store have similar language in their agreements. Barnes & Noble "reserves the right to modify or discontinue the offering of any Digital Content at any time." Apple's terms and conditions state that "You acknowledge that iTunes is selling you a license to use the content made available through the iBookstore" for your iPad (Brown 2012). The Kindle, NOOK or iPad owner does not own the content on the e-reader. The owner is simply agreeing to a license, which allows access to the content.

Reading agreements before signing is extremely important. The Sony license agreement states, "by accepting these Terms of Service, you are granted a non-exclusive, non-transferable, non-sublicensable, limited right to use the Service solely for the purposes of downloading, reading, listening to, and viewing Content in connection with the Service" (Sony Electronics 2012). The Kobo terms of service read, "you are granted a limited license to access the Service and the Site Content and to download or print a copy of any portion of the Site Content to which you have properly gained access solely for your personal, non-commercial use, provided that you keep all copyright and other proprietary notices intact" (Kobo, Inc. n.d.-b). Notice that both agreements stress "personal" and "non-transferable" use.

First Sale for Ebooks, Maybe—Someday?

Capitol records sued ReDigi, a music resale service, for infringement of copyright law. ReDigi sells digital music files that they remove from the seller's computer and then offer for sale at the ReDigi site. Michael Farrell explained their services in an article published by the *Boston Globe*: "When someone signs up to use its service, the company places a software application on the user's computer that transfers songs into a cloud-based storage locker on the Web" (2012).

The antivirus-like software that ReDigi used searched the original computer and any other devices synced to that computer to make sure that the seller did not have any illegal copies of the original file. The software also verified that the copy being sold was the original file. The ruling in this case was in favor of Capitol Records. So for now, used digital music, ebooks, and films downloaded over the Internet cannot be resold.

Capitol Records contended that the file is rented, not owned by the purchaser. Consequently, the purchaser does not have the right to sell the file. For now, the justice system agrees with Capitol Records, but ReDigi is filing an appeal. The final verdict in this trial might determine the answer to the question: Does the First Sale Doctrine apply to digital music and ebooks?

Looking Ahead

Copyright laws dictate how librarians circulate resources, educate patrons, and select materials used to teach classes. The TEACH Act modified an over-restrictive element in DMCA. Now, by working to modify the less equitable aspects of the current copyright law, ALA is working hard to make sure that the best interests of librarians, library users, authors, and publishers are being served. All librarians can hope that changes to the copyright laws will continue to improve students' access to ebooks in the future.

15

Fast-Changing Landscape

The world of ebooks is among the most volatile in the digital arena today. Mergers, lawsuits, and technical innovations make it vitally important for librarians to stay informed about developments on the horizon. As with any nascent industry, especially a digital industry, there are bound to be growing pains, but, at the same time, the new development of tomorrow may be the solution to today's challenges.

The magnitude of change in this arena is encapsulated by three news items appearing on one day in February 2013.

The U.S. Department of Justice approved a merger between Penguin and Random House.
Penguin has long been the poster child for volatility in the ebook universe; within one week in early November of 2011 Penguin precipitously pulled all titles out of OverDrive citing " security concerns," and then, in just a few days, dove back into OverDrive. A few weeks later Penguin pulled its titles from

OverDrive for good (Albanese 2011). The merger approved by the Department of Justice raises questions, as Penguin and Random House have had different approaches to ebooks in the past. While Penguin was doing its "Will we/Won't we?" dance with OverDrive, Random House has been happy to sell titles to OverDrive for library consumption at prices up to 300 percent of retail prices (Coldewey 2012). So far, there is no indication of what the merged companies will do. Will "Penguin Random House" pull previous Random House titles out of OverDrive? Will previously unincluded Penguin titles now be added to OverDrive? More will be revealed, so stay tuned! (Monroe 2013).

Webooks, created by the Genesee Valley Educational Partnership School Library System, Le Roy, N.Y., is presented as a creative solution for ebook purchases by a consortium of public school districts.

In recognizing Genesee Valley Educational Partnership School Library System's Webooks as a Cutting Edge Technology in Library Services, the American Library Association said "The library system created a website that allowed librarians across 22 school districts to pool together a portion of their individual library materials aid while maintaining control over spending through a participatory selection process" (Roberts 2013). This creative problem-solving is an example of the ways individuals, librarians, and school districts are banding together to address the challenges of ebook collection development. As more pioneers start developing solutions to specific problems, librarians from across the country can follow their lead (Harris 2013b). Indeed, this type of collaboration has gone one step further in the process of making ebooks available to school libraries with the launch of a new program called "Here Be Fiction" in limited beta format as of July 2013. Developed by the Genesee Valley Educational Partnership, Mackin and *School Library Journal,* this new endeavor will provide previews and reviews along with access to ebooks on terms that address school libraries' particular needs (Harris 2013a).

Developed in partnership with Colorado's Douglas County Libraries (DCL), Impelsys announces release of their new eBook Ordering System, allowing a library's collection development and acquisition staff to work directly with ebook publishers without a third-party ordering system.

With the development of its eBook Ordering System, Impelsys demonstrates the possibilities of industry partnering with libraries to create solutions to the seemingly immovable roadblocks between libraries and publishers. In its mission statement, Impelsys describes its goal as "delivering the most innovative, cost-effective, and flexible online content delivery technologies and services to the global publishing industry." By partnering with Douglas County Libraries, Impelsys teamed with an innovative force working to approach the confluence of ebooks, libraries, and publishers from a fresh new direction. The possibilities envisioned by Jamie LaRue and his colleagues when they published their "Colorado Ebook Manifesto" (2012) are now becoming a more fully developed reality as tools such as this are being created and brought to the market (Price 2013a).

These are just three examples of ebook news that happened to break on one day in February 2013, but they are indications of the variety and magnitude of change that is occurring in today's ebook ecosystem. One spectacular merger between major publishers, a new use of technology adapted by public school libraries specifically for ebooks in school libraries, and the introduction of a possible advance on the road to ebook independence away from the ironclad restrictions of the Big Six publishers—not a bad day's harvest of news, by any standard.

Demise of a Platform

When Fictionwise launched in June of 2000 it was part of the brave new world of electronic books, fast becoming one of the largest sellers of ebooks on the market. In 2009, when it was acquired by Barnes & Noble (B&N), it seemed poised to become a strong part of that company's digital portfolio. Over time, however, Fictionwise became less prominent as B&N developed other areas of ebook sales and management structured around the NOOK, and in December of 2012 came the announcement of the site's impending demise. In accordance with their contract, B&N gave their customers ninety days' notice that the site was to be shut down. Customers who used Fictionwise to purchase and manage their ebooks now found that it wasn't so easy to transfer their titles over to the Nook Store as B&N offered. For some the transfer went smoothly, but others were less successful. Imagine having hundreds of ebook titles in Fictionwise, only to find that only a small fraction were able to transfer properly. These are books that were bought and paid for through Fictionwise. Some readers found that less than 10 percent of their Fictionwise titles were transferrable to the NOOK Book Store. As recently as May 1, 2013, customers were still waiting for their transfers of legally purchased titles to be completed (Bookwurm70 2013).

In the case of non-U.S. customers, that number is zero percent, because B&N didn't make the transfer opportunity available to those outside of the United States. Not every case was problematic, but the idea that ebooks legally purchased would become unavailable due to technical change is one that prompts concern (Hoffelder 2012).

Those who were prepared for this situation managed to come through fine, having backed their books up beforehand. This backup process may have been illegal, at least in the cases of titles protected by DRM; however, the alternative of having a legally purchased title taken away by technological or business whim seems to prompt creative solutions.

Positive Change

Not all changes are negative. In the spring of 2013, as a result of a change in policy, Macmillan began selling ebooks to libraries; the limited pilot program involved 1,200 titles from Macmillan's Minotaur crime fiction backlist. The good news here is that one of the Big Six is selling ebooks to libraries, and at $25 per copy the cost is only expensive, not exorbitant. The bad news is that there are restrictions; each copy will last two years or fifty-two circulations, whichever comes first. To end with good news, though, that "two years or fifty-two circulations" rule offers a 100 percent improvement over the twenty-six circulations limit imposed by HarperCollins on ebooks it sells to libraries. (Robertson 2013).

Hopeful Signs

Digital music went through much of its growing pains through the late 1990s and early 2000s, when individual sales, downloading and sharing, piracy, Napster and iTunes all played a part in how the music industry came to develop its parameters for selling and using digital music. During that transformative process, the music industry came through inherently changed but with new vitality. *Billboard* reported "Overall Digital Sales (albums plus track-equivalent albums) up 10.4% year over year in the first 10 months of 2012" (Hampp et al.). In the early days of digital music, when the music industry was trying to beat back the specters of Napster and Freenet at their door, it would have been inconceivable to predict a 10 percent increase in sales for digital music. Data showing brick-and-mortar sales declining "are just evidence of the continuing transition to the digital marketplace" (Hampp et al. 2012).

Publisher concerns about security have driven ebook development toward rigid DRM-based restrictions with the aim of limiting the potential for piracy. With the passage of time, however, it is becoming apparent that this concern may be misplaced. In April of 2012, Tor Books, the world's leading publisher of science fiction, announced that it would no longer sell ebooks with DRM restrictions. These restrictions were seen as a serious annoyance to Tor's customers, who found themselves blocked from some important –and completely legal-- actions, including moving their books from one device to another. After almost a year of working completely without DRM, Tor published a report of their experience. "Julie Crisp, editorial director at Tor UK, wrote that the publisher has seen 'no discernible increase in piracy on any of our titles, despite them being DRM-free for nearly a year'" (Geuss 2013).

Another example of a positive development comes from BookExpo America 2013, which hosted a panel discussion titled: "Is E-book Lending Good for Authors, or Does it Lead to Lost Book Sales?" Present were OverDrive's CEO Steve Potash, Simon & Schuster's Carolyn Reidy, and Maureen Sullivan, 2012-2013 ALA president, among others. Paige Crutcher of *Publisher's Weekly* covered the discussion. "The session kicked off with general agreement that e-book lending is not only good for libraries but for authors and publishers too… discoverability was seen as one of the finer points of e-book lending" (2013). Jack Perry, owner of 38enso, sees the future in OverDrive's Big Library Read pilot program. "Libraries worldwide offer a single e-book to their patrons. The program spotlights a title for a set time period for library patrons to read simultaneously. Michael Malone is the first author to participate in the program with his novel *The Four Corners of the Sky*. In two weeks 37,100 readers have borrowed the book, the cover has had 5.9 million impressions, and visibility has increased 600 percent." This program, set to benefit authors, publishers AND libraries, is a prime example of creativity being applied to the balance of rights and access (Crutcher 2013).

It took the music industry at least ten years to adapt to the new digital paradigm, with the result of a restructured business model and thriving sales. Ebook publishers can learn from the music industry's experiences and save themselves — and librarians along with their students — some of these growing pains along the way.

Musings
Larger Philosophical Questions, Future Challenges, Concerns, and Developments

Lessons from the Past

One of the primary questions of the ebook ecosystem is that of ownership. With print books, the buyers own the books and can do with them what they will, subject to very limited copyright restrictions. The library landscape was designed with these parameters in mind; books could be bought, lent, weeded, given away. If more copies were needed to address demand, more copies were purchased.

As discussed earlier, the use of ebooks, as guided by DMCA, is very different. Generally speaking, when one purchases an ebook, one has purchased the license to use that ebook, for a longer or shorter period, with fewer or more restrictions on its use. Librarians are no longer the ultimate arbiter of the management of a library resource. Limits on the above functions — purchase, loan, and de-accession — are all tightly restricted by the EULA — the fine print of the "I Agree" statement.

Part of the problem some are having in understanding the world of ebooks arises from precisely this difference. The library landscape evolved over time to function optimally in a print environment.

Librarians must address rapid changes that our library programs have not yet evolved to deal with.

There is one area that might hold the key to understanding how libraries and ebooks can begin to coexist productively. In the 1980s and 1990s, with the development of periodical databases in various formats, a library's print periodicals were joined by electronic periodicals. Periodical databases provided increasingly flexible searchability, and, as full text became the norm, an additional benefit was making shelf space available for other resources. School libraries began to depend more on periodical databases for basic access to titles, and then began to cut back first on the length of time they held on to print periodicals as an archive, and then on the number of print periodicals they received. Most libraries continue to purchase print magazines and journals for browsability and reader interest, but many have become largely dependent on periodical databases to make current titles and back issues available to their students, especially for research.

This shift has resulted in greater flexibility in use of space, as the shelves of old bound volumes of archived periodicals were replaced by database access, and the square footage of current magazine display space was reduced. Increased searchability is an improvement as students can often search full text for topics that, in the past, could be located only by strictly controlled subject headings in the *Readers' Guide to Periodical Literature*.

One of the trade-offs for these improvements was the abdication of some elements of librarians' control of periodical management. If librarians discard back issues of a certain title because the school's periodical database contains the past twenty years of that title, this is a good thing; they've just saved a large amount of shelf space with no loss of access. If the librarians then find, perhaps a number of years later, that the periodical database is trimming its past holdings and those years of that title are no longer available, then there is an unintended loss of coverage. When libraries became dependent on databases to provide access, librarians lost the ability to keep or toss back issues based on their own school's needs. If the database provider then decides that that title is no longer needed at all, that is the decision of the database provider and not the librarian.

Of course the librarian still has the power of the purse strings, and can register complaints with the database provider, perhaps engaging in discussion with the provider as to what the library needs. Ultimately, the librarian can drop that provider if service is unsatisfactory, and begin with another provider.

Librarians have been dealing with this set of parameters for years. They aren't generally concerned whether the school "owns" or "subscribes to" a certain magazine, as long as access is available. Librarians don't bemoan the fact that, as they've already paid for the print copies of the magazine, they then need to pay for the back issues every year with the renewal of the periodical database subscription. Librarians realize that for school library programs, the bottom line is access, not ownership.

The change in "ownership" of periodicals came over time. Eventually, librarians relinquished the precise control over periodical management in return for convenience and space. In most school libraries, the periodical world is now a mixture of print and digital, and that is acceptable to librarians and other stakeholders, particularly as they have worked with the periodical database vendors over the years and have built up a sense of understanding and trust.

As school library programs move into the realm of ebooks, it might help to see it as another shift similar to that which was experienced with periodicals. Librarians need to take time to understand the environment, get to know the vendors, and develop a sense of mutual benefit with them. This brave new world is not so different from changes that have occurred in the past.

Reader's Advisory

One area of emerging concern is "reader's advisory" or "patron interface." Many aspects of the library ebook experience can lead to fewer opportunities for students and librarians to interact. When ebooks are available for download through a vendor like OverDrive, that book never passes through the hands of the librarian, and the opportunity for discussion or questions, all part of developing a relationship, is lost. Particularly in the school environment, the sense of community that is built upon personal interactions is very important.

When ebooks are not physically on the shelf, "browsability" is adversely affected. Students depending on the library's organizational scheme to help them find similar materials next to each other on the shelf are out of luck. Those checking the shelves for intriguing fiction do not have that colorful package of marketing brilliance to pique their interest, and the librarian's tried and true methods of creative display and rotating book racks are not available in the ebook ecosystem.

It's true that you can't tell a book by its cover, but if it has no physical cover at all it can be difficult to find the book in the first place. Librarians are finding that reader's advisory services are still possible with ebooks; they just require more active promotion and energy. Increased outreach is necessary to teach students that the librarian is more helpful than ever before in guiding them to the materials they need.

Some vendors of the large library platforms like OverDrive and 3M Cloud offer a "discovery kiosk": a standalone station or wall-mounted station that allows interactive display to help patrons browse for titles. These are not cheap, but can be a useful means of combining search and display functions with content-management capability to allow downloading of selected ebooks to a student's device. A drawback to this model is the need to search each platform separately. A student must select a particular vendor's catalog to search, and then if the title is not available, the student must switch vendor platforms and search again. This is an area that may see improvements sooner rather than later, as technology is developing to integrate the discovery and circulation capabilities within a school's ILS. The technology isn't perfected yet, but advances in SIP2 (Standard Interchange Protocol 2) are on the horizon that could make such integration a reality.

Ebooks and Interlibrary Loan

Related to the issue of reader's advisory is interlibrary loan (ILL). This has been a vital service relied on by both public and school librarians to extend their collections beyond the physical walls of the library. It is a service that is made possible, as is most library lending, by the Right of First Purchase. Since the library owns the print copy of the book, it can lend the book at will. The difference between lending to local patrons and lending to those an ocean away is immaterial.

With ebooks, however, this service is stopped dead. DMCA dictates that the ebook cannot be legally copied, and it is impossible to lend an ebook without making a copy of it. There is some interest among today's entrepreneurs in developing software that would verify that the digital copy of the ebook was removed from the original server before being transferred to another server. One such service is called LightLibrary <http://lightlibrary.net>, which describes itself as "an iPhone-based application that allows you to get discounted e-book releases of the books you already own in print. We do this with a patent-pending, mobile-based process that verifies your book ownership." According to its COO, LightLibrary planned to roll out its first test releases in March 2013 (Oliver 2013), so it is very much a work in progress, but the effort is a sign that there are developments in this area that may soon show promise of solving some of the problems related to the equitable distribution of ebooks.

This activity is similar to what ReDigi tried to do with music, although ReDigi only works with music purchased legally through iTunes. Even with that limitation and arguably legal basis (the music was documented as legally purchased, and is transferred from the original purchaser, so no copy is made, at least according to ReDigi), legal troubles soon arose in the form of a lawsuit, *Capital Records, LLC v. ReDigi Inc.* On March 30, 2013, U.S. District Court Judge Richard Sullivan handed down a ruling in favor of Capital Records, leaving ReDigi the choice whether to appeal to the U.S. Supreme Court or to go back to the drawing board. To date, this software solution does not exist as applied to ebooks, and DRM remains firmly in place, blocking transfer of ebooks in most cases. Many publishers of popular fiction do not seem interested in using libraries as they did in the past to spread word about new authors and publications. This lost connection between best-selling authors, publishers, and libraries results in a real loss of service.

Hope may be waiting around the corner, however. One solution to the ILL conundrum might be developing as a result of the inventive approaches taken by some publishers and vendors. ProQuest's EBL is one example of a company working on new methods of ebook distribution, some versions of which might be seen as a viable stand-in for ILL. One such option is on the order of "Rent to Own," in which a book may be "rented" at a lower price for each circulation, with a trigger that kicks in to purchase that book at a particular number of circulations.

Admittedly, these are not precisely ILL procedures because the book is not sent from one library to another. However, if there are models for a relatively inexpensive "one time use" option, in effect a rental of a desired ebook, the practical result is much the same as it would be through ILL. A student can have the use of a desired ebook for one pseudo-circulation, and the price to the library is minimal. These creative new ways of considering ebook use and purchase are indications that solutions to the logjam of publisher restrictions might not be far away.

Publisher Concerns and Access Issues

Publishers and libraries have long enjoyed a productive, mutually beneficial working relationship. Along with bookstores, libraries traditionally have been prime locations for author tours and new-book promotions. While it is hard to quantify, experience shows that, for print titles, libraries serve as a valuable introduction to new titles and authors. In the past, a big chunk of publisher's book sales could trace their origins back to buyers learning about the author or title through their local libraries. With the number of brick and mortar bookstores continuing their decline due to the increasing impact of online sales through Amazon and others, this positive influence on book sales has become even more pronounced.

This relatively friendly history made many publishers' original position — limiting or blocking sales of ebooks to libraries—difficult for librarians to understand. It is important to note that publishers do not all agree on how to deal with libraries, and, in fact, most publishers of educational and reference materials are at the forefront of developing innovative ways of working with libraries for everyone's benefit, including the students'. Many publishers of popular fiction and nonfiction, however, have decided that the passage of DMCA has given them the opportunity to reconfigure their relationship with libraries. As digital books are very easy to copy compared with print books, and digital copies do not wear out or get lost, some publishers had decided that it was not good business to deal with libraries at all. These publishers' view is that putting their ebooks in libraries creates too much risk that those ebooks will be copied and pirated to the detriment of sales. Other publishers will sell to libraries but at 200 to 300 percent increase over prices for individual purchasers. Still other restrictions apply, including making the book expire—disappear from the catalog—after a set number of circulations, perhaps twenty-six in one year or fifty-two in two years. After the expiration is reached, the library must buy the book again or do without.

Penguin Random House has introduced some variables that may lead to a loosening of these restrictions. One early idea was that of "embargo" whereby a new book could be purchased in ebook format but only after a specified period of time—say six months from the publication date—has passed. This suggests a parallel to the movie industry, where a DVD of a movie is not released for sale until a specified period of time goes by after the opening of the movie. Hachette has developed a model that looks promising as a more balanced compromise between the needs of libraries and publishers. Hachette will make new titles available to libraries as ebooks at 300 percent of the original hardcover price, but that ebook will be available to that library in perpetuity, with no need to re-purchase it ever, under the one-user-one-copy model. There is the option to purchase the ebook one year after original publication at 150 percent of the current hardback price, also as a one-time purchase. While expensive at first, the offer of a choice in pricing (much like the difference between buying the hardcover copy or waiting to save money when it comes out in paperback) and the ability to count on a one-time purchase for continuing access both make this model an example of practical creativity (Enis 2013b).

This type of creative thinking may be a sign of light at the end of the tunnel, but unfortunately it is overshadowed by the fact that, as of March 2013, thirteen of the twenty-four NYT ebook best sellers (including fiction, nonfiction and children's) were entirely unavailable to libraries, and eight titles were available for as much as $84 (DCL 2013a). When publishers do agree to sell to libraries, they often try to build "friction" into the equation. Their fear is that it will be too easy to borrow an ebook, resulting in declining book sales to the detriment of publishers. As Jared Newman of *PCWorld* explains, "being able to download library ebooks is too easy" from the publisher's point of view. In fact, the inconvenience of getting ebooks from the library does not need to be artificially injected. "If you've ever actually tried to borrow a library ebook, however, you know that most of the friction comes from books being all checked out, not from the actual download process," says Newman (2012).In a way, though, this is no different than the hold process for popular print books, but at least in that case the library is free to manage their systems as they choose. As anyone who has tried to borrow a specific new ebook from a public library knows, the length of the wait list can be daunting. A parallel can be found with library management of popular new fiction print books, where reduced circulation periods allow for increased use of the book by more people. There are ways of managing high demand and still preserving publishers' rights.

It is to be hoped that as librarians and their patrons live with the realities of ebooks, libraries, publishers, and students will learn to coexist in mutually beneficial relationships. When they announced in April 2013 that they were no longer placing an embargo on new fiction titles sold to libraries, Penguin took a positive step toward solving the problems that have kept new ebooks out of the hands of students and patrons. "We are encouraged by Penguin's willingness to experiment, make adjustments and move forward with libraries and our millions of readers," American Library Association president Maureen Sullivan said in a statement obtained by the AP. Creative solutions like this will do much to bring back the positive, productive relationship that has long existed between publishers and libraries (Sullivan 2013b).

17

Conclusion

The electronic book presents perhaps the biggest challenge to libraries since the advent of automation. In the 1980s and early 1990s, librarians were scrambling to address the innovations and pitfalls of computers as they burst upon the scene. Automated catalogs, MARC coding, CD-ROM-based resources, circulation control—all those developments came even before the widespread access to the Internet. Those of us who were active in libraries in those days remember the combined excitement and panic we felt when trying to understand the changing landscape of school libraries. While automation and the Internet brought with them a certain amount of confusion and transitional bother, the advancements in delivering improved library services to our students is undeniable. In the same way, we are seeing great potential in the area of ebooks, but the story isn't fully told—we don't yet know the ending.

A major conundrum that must be solved is the fact that libraries cannot legally purchase the most popular titles in ebook format. The team at Douglas County Libraries (DCL) have made a practice of posting monthly data regarding ebooks and libraries. The data from March 4, 2013, looking at ebook access to the twenty-four titles on *The New York Times* Best Seller List, including children's/young adult offerings, show that only eleven of the titles on the list, fewer than half, are available for sale to libraries at all. Out of those eleven titles, eight ranged in price from $47.85 to $80.85 per copy; the other three were priced at under $17.00. These are in comparison to titles that sell to consumers for as little as $.99, ranging up to $12.99 (DCL 2013a). When looking at the twenty top circulating titles at DCL during the month of February 2013, the situation was worse. Jamie LaRue stated the unfortunate truth: Out of these twenty titles, only five were available for sale as ebooks to libraries, and those cost "almost twice the price [compared to consumer prices] at best, six and a half times greater at worst" (LaRue and Harris 2013).

These are titles from *The New York Times* Best Seller List, and circulation statistics from a large public library, so it is true that there are some differences when looking at practices at school libraries. Because one major way our students use our collections is for research, we have the advantage that more of our nonfiction and academic titles are available to us in ebook format through the vendors discussed in these pages. That advantage, however, doesn't alleviate the concern that so much popular fiction remains largely unavailable to our students in ebook format through the school library. This is an area in urgent need of improvement.

In response to this need on the part of libraries everywhere, the International Federation of Library Associations (IFLA), met in November 2012 to work on recommendations to advance the cause of library access to ebooks. Years of talks between librarians and publishers in Sweden, Denmark and Germany in particular had broken down with no positive results, and librarians needed to come together to decide on new approaches. Against the backdrop of failed negotiations such as these, some points of light give hope of advancement. Peter Brantley of *Publishers Weekly* reported on the main success story of the conference. "Canada represented the most successful alliance between libraries and publishers. Two years of negotiations with the Association of Canadian Publishers has resulted in a landmark draft proposal for licensing a bundle of e-books, with terms loosely based on the HarperCollins model but good for 40 loans over 5 years" (2013). It is to be noted that this agreement was launched with government support, indicating the amount of heavy lifting required to push this type of proposal through. Still, it is a positive development, and one that may serve as a model in future negotiations between librarians and publishers.

Having immersed ourselves in the ebook universe during the writing of this book, we are firmly convinced that, for all the challenges facing us, the future of school libraries will be a healthy mix of print and digital sources, but we need to proceed carefully. There is no shortage of examples of those diving into the digital deep end, with mixed results. A recent *Publishers Weekly* article trumpeted the arrival of "The Bookless Library," in reference to BiblioTech, a brand new library in Bexar County, Texas. Closer examination reveals a situation that seems to result in a library lacking important resources. *Publishers Weekly*'s Peter Brantley again weighs in on the world of ebooks, this time in obvious admiration of the prospect of a bookless library. He does make the observation that "no digital library can be comprehensive today because of publisher reluctance to license their books," and reports County Judge Nelson W. Wolff's response. "He readily acknowledged that *not all literature could be presented to county residents* through an ebook platform [emphasis mine]. Yet, he was hopeful that forward-looking demonstrations of community libraries such as BiblioTech would encourage publishers to enlarge their offerings, reaching readers that lacked any bookstore." Bexar County is taking the step of creating a library with a serious lack of resources in the stated hope that publishers will someday broaden their policies. It would be foolish and indeed irresponsible to jettison practical print resources in search of either additional space or the reputation for cutting-edge technology, trumpeting sweeping changes but reducing service and access. For all the pioneer spirit displayed, it is no accident that a stated motivation of Bexar County is the "cost-effective strategy" of going completely digital.

Are we in danger of becoming a bookless society? The answer, according to any number of surveys, is a resounding NO. A Pew Internet survey released in June 2013 titled "Younger Americans'

Library Habits and Expectations" paints a healthy scenario of print and digital reading among young people.

> As with other age groups, younger Americans were significantly more likely to have read an e-book during 2012 than a year earlier. Among all those ages 16-29, 19% read an e-book during 2011, while 25% did so in 2012. **At the same time, however, print reading among younger Americans has remained steady: When asked if they had read at least one print book in the past year, the same proportion (75%) of Americans under age 30 said they had both in 2011 and in 2012.**
>
> In fact, younger Americans under age 30 are now significantly more likely than older adults to have read a book in print in the past year (75% of all Americans ages 16-29 say this, compared with 64% of those ages 30 and older). And more than eight in ten (85%) older teens ages 16-17 read a print book in the past year, making them significantly more likely to have done so than any other age group. (Zickuhr et al. 2013).

We said in the Introduction that we are looking forward to a time when the format of a book is irrelevant; the content, story, characters, and scene are what we talk about, not whether it was delivered in print or digital format, was an audiobook or paperback. In fact, we've seen a similar revolution in format, with admittedly fewer complications but with a similar concern for the future of our cultural development. The "Paperback Revolution" of the early- to mid-1900s was seen by many as cause for concern. As American author Harvey Swados observed, in 1951:

> "Whether this revolution in the reading habits of the American public means that we are being inundated by a flood of trash which will debase farther the popular taste, or that we shall now have available cheap editions of an ever-increasing list of classics, is a question of basic importance to our social and cultural development." – *Harvey Swados, 1951* quoted at The Paperback Revolution.

History tells us that the American public and the American library weathered the storm of the "Paperback Revolution" quite handily. We are betting on a similar result with the Ebook Revolution. The question should not be "Print or digital—either/or?" with the limitations inherent in that comparison; the reality will be "both/and," with the broad spectrum of access that suggests. Our students deserve no less.

 WORKS CITED

3M. 2006. *3M Standard Interchange Protocol*, Rev. 2.12. <http://multimedia.3m.com/mws/mediawebserver?6666660Zjcf6lVs6EVs66S0LeCOrrrQ-> (accessed March 29, 2013).

Abarbanel, Elisabeth. 2013. Personal e-mail correspondence. Head Librarian. Brentwood School, East Campus. January 24.

Acedo, Shannon. 2013. Personal experience.

Adobe Systems Software Ireland Ltd. 2013. "Adobe Digital Editions Home." <www.adobe.com/au/products/digital-editions.html> (accessed February 16, 2013).

Albanese, Andrew. 2011. "Citing 'Security Concerns', Penguin pulls new titles out of OverDrive." *Publishers Weekly* (November 21). <www.publishersweekly.com/pw/by-topic/digital/content-and-e-books/article/49598-citing-security-concerns-penguin-pulls-new-titles-from-overdrive.html> (accessed June 6, 2013).

Alfred, Randy. 2008. "Oct. 28, 1998: President Signs New Copyright Law." *Wired* (October 28, 2008). <www.wired.com/science/discoveries/news/2008/10/dayintech_1028> (accessed May 10, 2013).

Alvarez, Edgar. 2012. "Tablet Maker Pandigital No Longer Offering Warranty Replacements, Reminds Us It's Now Out of Business." <www.engadget.com/2012/11/21/pandigital-out-of-business> (accessed May 11, 2013).

Amazon.com, Inc. 2013a. "The World's Best Selling E-readers." <http://www.amazon.com/gp/product/B008UB7DU6/ref=fs_clw#tech> (accessed January 2, 2013).

———. 2013b. "Terms of Use." <http://services.amazon.com/content/Terms_Conditions.htm?ld=AZFSSOA> (accessed May 11, 2013).

———. 2013c. "Kindle Fire Device and Feature Specifications." <https://developer.amazon.com/sdk/fire/specifications.html> (accessed June 4, 2013).

American Association of School Librarians. 2009. *Empowering Learners: Guidelines for School Library Programs*. Chicago: ALA.

American Library Association. 2013. "DMCA: The Digital Millennium Copyright Act." <www.ala.org/advocacy/copyright/dmca> (accessed February 19, 2013).

Android. n.d. [about page] <www.android.com/about> (accessed February 2, 2013).

Apple Inc. 2010. "Apple Launches iPad." <www.apple.com/pr/library/2010/01/27Apple-Launches-iPad.html> (accessed April 19, 2013).

———. 2012. "iBooks Author Support." <http://www.apple.com/support/ibooksauthor/> (accessed August 31, 2012).

———. 2013a. "Apple Awarded $30 Million iPad Deal From LA Unified School District." <http://www.apple.com/pr/library/2013/06/19Apple-Awarded-30-Million-iPad-Deal-From-LA-Unified-School-District.html> (accessed July 1, 2013).

———. 2013b. "iOS: The World's Most Advanced Operating System." <www.apple.com/iphone/ios> (accessed February 2, 2013).

———. 2013c. "iPad mini: Every Inch an iPad." <www.apple.com/ipad-mini/overview> (accessed March 29, 2013).

Bane, Katie. 2012. "3M Cloud Library eBook Lending Service." *American Libraries* (May 14). < http://americanlibrariesmagazine.org/solutions-and-services/3m-cloud-library-ebook-lending-service> (accessed June 3, 2012).

Barnesandnoble.com LLC. 2013a. "NOOK HD." <http://
www.barnesandnoble.com/p/nook-hd-barnes-noble/
1110060426#nook-commentary-features-1> (accessed January 2,
2013).

———. 2013b."NOOK Simple Touch." < http://www.
barnesandnoble.com/p/nook-simple-touch-barnes-noble/
1102344735#nook-commentary-features-1> (accessed January 2,
2013).

———. 2013c. "Terms and Conditions of Use." <www.
barnesandnoble.com/include/terms_of_use.asp> (accessed
February 12, 2013>.

Bauer, Stephen M. 2005. "Students with Learning Disabilities:
Reading." Assistive Technology Training Online Project (ATTO).
University of Buffalo. <http://atto.buffalo.edu/registered/
ATBasics/Populations/LD/reading.php> (accessed May 30,
2013).

Begun, Daniel A. 2013. "Looking at the Android Operating System."
<www.dummies.com/how-to/content/looking-at-the-android-
operating-system0.html> (accessed March 28, 2013).

Behler, Anne. 2011. "E-Book Tip Sheets: Collection Development for
E-Books." <www.ala.org/offices/sites/ala.org.offices/files/
content/oitp/ebook_collection_dev.pdf> (accessed January 14,
2013).

Bills, Michael. 2013. Personal e-mail correspondence. Director for
Sales, Digital Products. Baker & Taylor. February 22.

———. 2013. Personal e-mail correspondence. June 5.

Bluefire Productions, LLC. 2011. "Two Kind Words for eBook Lovers:
Bluefire Reader." <www.bluefirereader.com/bluefire-reader.
html> (accessed May 8, 2013).

Bookwurm70. 2013. "Fictionwise Book Transfer." *Mobileread
Forum* (May 1). <www.mobileread.com/forums/showthread.ph
p?t=212070&highlight=fictionwise+transfer%2A> (accessed June
6, 2013).

Brain Hive, LLC. 2012. "Brain Hive: eBooks on Demand for K–12 Libraries." <www.brainhive.com/Pages/Home.aspx> (accessed March 28, 2013).

Braniff, Amanda. 2010. "Collection Development Policy." Denver: Montessori School of Denver.

Brantley, Peter. 2013. "Digital Lending, In Agreement." *PWxyz* (January 6). <http://blogs.publishersweekly.com/blogs/PWxyz/2013/01/06/digital-lending-in-agreement> (accessed January 18, 2013).

Brown, Eileen. 2012. "Why Amazon Is within Its Rights to Remove Access to Your Kindle Books." *ZDNet* (October 25). <www.zdnet.com/why-amazon-is-within-its-rights-to-remove-access-to-your-kindle-books-7000006385> (accessed February 21, 2013).

Burliegh, David. 2013. Personal e-mail correspondence. Director of Marketing. OverDrive. June 15.

Cabiness, Marvin. 2013. Personal e-mail correspondence. Territory Manager, Salem Press. March 13.

Capstone. 2011a. "Capstone Interactive Library." <www.capstonepub.com/content/DIGITAL_CIL> (accessed March 28, 2013).

———. 2011b. "Capstone Interactive Library: Learn More." <www.capstonepub.com/content/DIGITAL_CIL#LearnMore> (accessed May 2, 2013).

———. 2011c. "myON reader." <www.capstonepub.com/content/DIGITAL_MYON> (accessed May 2, 2013).

Colao, J. J. 2012. "Apple's Biggest (Unknown) Supplier of E-Books." *Forbes*. <www.forbes.com/sites/jjcolao/2012/06/07/apples-biggest-unknown-supplier-of-e-books/> (accessed June 5, 2013).

Coldewey, Devin. 2012. "Necessary Evil? Random House Triples Prices of Library E-Books." *TeleCrunch* (March 2). <http://techcrunch.com/2012/03/02/necessary-evil-random-house-triples-prices-of-library-e-books/> (accessed June 6, 2013).

Credo Corporation. n.d.-a. "Literati School: School Core." <http://corp.credoreference.com/solutions/literati-school/content/school-core.html> (accessed June 5, 2013).

———. n.d.-b. "Credo Online Reference Service." <http://corp.
credoreference.com/solutions/credo-online-reference-service.
html> (accessed June 5, 2013).

Crumm, Chris. 2012. "Barnes & Noble Continues Nook Expansion
in UK." *Web Pro News.* <www.webpronews.com/barnes-noble-
continues-nook-expansion-in-uk-2012-09> (accessed March 23,
2013).

Crumm, Erin. 2013. Personal e-mail correspondence. Vice President,
Corporate Communications at HarperCollins. January 17.

Digital Public Library of America. 2012. "ELEMENTS OF THE
DPLA." <http://blogs.law.harvard.edu/dplaalpha/about/
elements-of-the-dpla/> (accessed March 09, 2013).

Dimpsey, Beth. 2011. "ebrary Launches the Industry's First Usage-
Triggered Model for Short-Term Loans." Ebrary Press Release.
(May 2) <www.ebrary.com/corp/newspdf/ebrary_STL.pdf>
(accessed June 3, 2013).

Doctorow, Cory. 2012. "Kindle User Claims Amazon Deleted Whole
Library without Explanation." *BoingBoing* (October 22). <http://
boingboing.net/2012/10/22/kindle-user-claims-amazon-dele.
html> (accessed April 12, 2013).

Douglas County Libraries. 2012a. "An Open Letter about eBooks and
Douglas County Libraries." <http://douglascountylibraries.org/
content/ebooks-and-DCL> (accessed May 7, 2013).

———. 2012b. "Douglas County Libraries Report: Pricing
Comparison as of October 31, 2012." <http://evoke.cvlsites.org/
files/2012/10/DCLPriceReportOct-31-12.pdf> (accessed March
31, 2013).

———. 2013a. "Douglas County Libraries Report: Pricing
Comparison as of March 4, 2013." <http://evoke.cvlsites.org/
files/2013/03/DCL-Pricing-Comparison-3-4-13.pdf> (accessed
March 17, 2013).

———.2013b. "Douglas County Libraries Report: Pricing Comparison
as of June 3, 2013." <http://evoke.cvlsites.org/files/2013/06/
DCL-Pricing-Comparison-6-3-13.pdf> (accessed June 17, 2013).

———. 2013c. "Statement of Common Understanding for Purchasing Electronic Content." <http://evoke.cvlsites.org/files/2012/03/CommonUnderstandingPurchaseEbooks2012Jan11.pdf> (accessed January 18, 2013).

"Ebook Timeline." 2002.*The Guardian* (January 3). <http://www.guardian.co.uk/books/2002/jan/03/ebooks.technology> (accessed May28, 2013).

ebrary, a ProQuest Business. n.d. "ebrary for High Schools." <www.ebrary.com/corp/schools.jsp> (accessed June 17, 2013).

EBSCO Industries, Inc. 2012. "Don't Federate. Integrate: A Next-Generation Approach to Federation." <www.ebscohost.com/academic/ebscohost-integrated-search> (accessed January 12, 2013).

———. n.d.-a. "EBSCO Discovery Service Support Center." <http://support.epnet.com/eds/> (accessed June 3, 2013).

———. n.d.-b. "Patron Driven Acquisition." <www.ebscohost.com/ebooks/patron-driven-acquisition> (accessed March 29, 2013).

Electronic Frontier Foundation. n.d. "DRM." <www.eff.org/issues/drm> (accessed January 18, 2013).

Ellis, Leanne. 2013. Personal e-mail correspondence. Library Coordinator. New York City School Library Services. January 11.

Enis, Matt. 2013a. "Califa Launches Enki, a Lending Platform for Direct Ebook Distribution." *The Digital Shift* (May 20). <www.thedigitalshift.com/2013/05/ebooks/califa-launches-enki-a-lending-platform-for-direct-ebook-distribution/> (accessed June 4, 2013).

———. 2013b. "Hachette to Sell Frontlist Ebook Titles to Libraries." *The Digital Shift* (May 1). <http://www.thedigitalshift.com/2013/05/ebooks/hachette-to-sell-frontlist-ebook-titles-to-libraries/> (accessed June 4).

Farrell, Michael B. 2012. "Case Could Pave Way for Reselling Digital Music, Other Products." *Boston Globe* (July 2). <www.bostonglobe.com/business/2012/07/01/the-used-record-store-goes-digital-music-resale-brings-digital-showdown/

vOhr7pzVNiWc2gRjKa9EnN/story.html> (accessed March 9, 2013).

Fictionwise. 2013. "FAQ Page—Fictionwise Bookshelf Transfer to Barnes & Noble's NOOK Library." <www.fictionwise.com/BN-Transition-FAQ.htm> (accessed February 14, 2013).

Follansbee, Joe. 2011. Quoted by "Tony" in "Small Ebook Publishers Apparently Excluded from Amazon/OverDrive Deal with Libraries for Kindle Ebook Lending." *EbookAnoid* (November 2). <www.ebookanoid.com/2011/11/02/small-ebook-publishers-apparently-excluded-from-amazonoverdrive-deal-with-libraries-for-kindle-ebook-lending> (accessed November 18, 2012).

Follett. 2013. "FolletShelf: eContent Anywhere. Anytime." <http://www.aboutfollettebooks.com/follettshelf.cfm> (accessed June 29, 2013).

Frank, Maureen. 2013. Personal e-mail correspondence. Librarian. Harvard-Westlake Upper School. June 6.

Freeman, Dan. 2013. Personal e-mail correspondence. Online Learning Manager. American Library Association (ALA). April 1.

Gardner, Eileen, and Ronald G. Musto. 2010. "The Electronic Book." In *Oxford Companion to the Book*, edited by Michael Suarezz and H. R. Woudhuysen, Vol. 1, 164–71. Oxford: Oxford University Press.

Geuss, Megan. 2013. "Tor Books Says Cutting DRM Out of its E-Books Hasn't Hurt Business." *Ars Technica* (May 4). <http://arstechnica.com/business/2013/05/tor-books-says-cutting-drm-out-of-its-e-books-hasnt-hurt-business/> (accessed 6/10/2013).

Google. n.d. -a. "Google Books History." <www.google.com/googlebooks/about/history.html> (accessed March 27, 3013).

———. n.d. -b. "Nexus 7." <www.google.com/nexus/7> (accessed March 29, 2013).

———. n.d. -c. "Our History in Depth." <http://www.google.com/about/company/history/> (accessed April 19, 2013).

Guagliardo, John. 2013. Personal e-mail correspondence. Executive Director. World Public Library. June 6.

Hamilton, Buffy. 2012. "Choosing an E-Book Platform That Works for Your K12 Library." <www.slideshare.net/buffyjhamilton/choosing-an-ebook-platform-that-works-for-your-k12-library-13917868> (accessed August 28, 2012).

Hampp, Andrew, et al. 2012. "100+ Platforms That Move Music Now." *Billboard* 124 (39): 20–31.

Harris, Christopher. 2013a. "'Here Be Fiction' Launches: New Site Features Ebook Fiction Available to Schools on Library-Friendly Terms". *The Digital Shift* (June 28). <http://www.thedigitalshift.com/2013/06/opinion/the-next-big-thing/here-be-fiction-launches-new-site-features-ebook-fiction-available-to-schools-on-library-friendly-terms-the-next-big-thing/> (accessed June 28, 2013).

———. 2013b. "Webooks: A Novel Plan for Cooperative Ebook Purchasing: The Next Big Thing." *The Digital Shift* (February 14). <www.thedigitalshift.com/2013/02/opinion/the-next-big-thing/ebook-crowdsourcing-an-award-winning-plan-for-cooperative-purchasing-the-next-big-thing> (accessed April 1, 2013).

Hastings, Jeff. 2011. "School Library Loans Via Kindle: Jeff Hastings Weighs in on OverDrive's Partnership with Amazon." *School Library Journal* (June 1). <www.libraryjournal.com/slj/printissue/currentissue/890548-427/school_library_loans_via_kindle.html.csp> (accessed January 10, 2013).

———. 2012. "Ebook Toolkit: Mackin VIA." *The Digital Shift* (June 4). <www.thedigitalshift.com/2012/06/ebooks/ebook-toolkit-mackin-via> (accessed April 11, 2013).

HathiTrust. 2008. "Launch of HathiTrust—October 13, 2008." <www.hathitrust.org/press_10-13-2008> (accessed April 1, 2013).

———. 2012. "HathiTrust Statement on Authors Guild v. HathiTrust Ruling." <www.hathitrust.org/authors_guild_lawsuit_ruling> (accessed April 1, 2013).

Hoffelder, Nate. 2012. "B&N Could Only Transfer One in Ten of My eBooks from Fictionwise to NOOK." *Digital Reader* (November 16). <www.the-digital-reader.com/2012/11/16/bn-offers-an-

easy-way-to-transfer-ebooks-from-fictionwise-to-the-nook-store-but-it-doesnt-work/#comment-82222> (accessed May 11, 2013).

Impelsys. 2009. "About Us." <www.impelsys.com/aboutus> (accessed May 11, 2013).

Ingram Content Group, Inc. n.d. "MyiLibrary: Gain, Retain and Share Knowledge." <www.myilibrary.com> (accessed March 9, 2013).

International Children's Digital Library. 2013. "Library Fast Facts." <http://en.childrenslibrary.org/about/fastfacts.shtml> (accessed April 19, 2013).

International Digital Publishing Forum. 2012. "EPUB." <http://www.idpf.org/epub/30/spec/epub30-overview.html> (accessed December 31, 2012).

International Federation of Library Associations and Institutions. 2013. "IFLA Principles for Library eLending." <www.ifla.org/node/7418> (accessed May 9, 2013).

Jaime W. 2013. "New to Ebooks? Start Here." *Free Library Blog* (May 7). <http://libwww.freelibrary.org/blog/index.cfm?postid=1739> (accessed June 16, 2013).

ITHAKA. 2012. [JSTOR books homepage]. <http://books.jstor.org> (accessed March 2, 2013).

Jaime W. 2013. "New to Ebooks? Start Here." *Free Library Blog* (May 7). <http://libwww.freelibrary.org/blog/index.cfm?postid=1739> (accessed June 16, 2013).

Kaufman, Leslie. 2012. "Penguin to Expand E-Book Lending." *Media Decoder: Behind the Scenes between the Times* (November 18). <http://mediadecoder.blogs.nytimes.com/2012/11/18/penguin-to-expand-e-book-lending> (accessed January 3, 2013).

Kelley, Michael. 2012. "One Year Later, HarperCollins Sticking to 26-Loan Cap, and Some Librarians Rethink Opposition." *The Digital Shift* (February 17). <www.thedigitalshift.com/2012/02/ebooks/one-year-later-harpercollins-sticking-to-26-loan-cap-and-some-librarians-rethink-opposition/> (accessed May 30, 2013).

———. 2013. "Top Ebook Distributors, ILS Vendors to Have Sitdown With ReadersFirst Library Coalition." *The Digital Shift* (January

3). <www.thedigitalshift.com/2013/01/ebooks/top-ebook-distributors-ils-vendors-to-have-sitdown-with-readersfirst-library-coalition> (accessed January 11, 2013).

Kelly, Roger. 2013. Personal e-mail correspondence. Youth Services Coordinator. Santa Monica Public Library. January 5.

King, David Lee. 2013. "The Big Six: Where We Stand At The Moment." David Lee King (May 21). <http://www.davidleeking.com/2013/05/21/the-big-six-where-we-stand-at-the-moment/> (accessed June 16, 2013).

K-NFB Reading Technology, Inc. 2010. "K-NFB Reading Technology." <www.knfbreader.com> (accessed December 30, 2012).

Kno Inc. 2013a. "About Us." <www.kno.com/corp> (accessed April 30, 2013).

———. 2013b. [features page]. <www.kno.com/features> (accessed April 30, 2013).

Kobo Inc. n.d.-a. "Kobo Arc: Designed for Readers, Perfect for Everything." <www.kobo.com/koboarc> (accessed March 29, 2013).

——— n.d.-b. "Kobobooks.com: Terms of Use." <www.kobobooks.com/termsofuse> (accessed February 25, 2013).

——— n.d.-c. "Frequently Asked Questions: Everything You Wanted To Know About Kobo Mini." <http://www.kobo.com/kobomini/support/> (accessed June 4, 2013).

Krug, Ken. 2012. Personal e-mail correspondence. Vendor representative. FollettShelf. October 31.

LaRue, Jamie. 2012. "Colorado Ebook Manifesto." <http://jaslarue.blogspot.com/2012/07/colorado-ebook-manifesto.html> (accessed November 18, 2012).

LaRue, Jamie. 2013a. "The Rise and Fall of Digital Independence and Self-Publishing." *ForeWord Reviews* (Spring 2013). <www.forewordreviews.com/articles/article/the-rise-and-fall-of-digital-independence-and-self-publishing/> (accessed June 4, 2013).

————. 2013b. "An Open Letter About eBooks and Douglas County Libraries." <http://douglascountylibraries.org/content/ebooks-and-DCL> (accessed June 4, 2013).

LaRue, Jamie, and Christopher Harris. 2013. "What's 'Selling' at the Library: February 2013 Ebook Report from DCL." *American Libraries* (February 4). <www.americanlibrariesmagazine.org/blog/what's-"selling"-library-february-2013-ebook-report-dcl> (accessed June 24, 2013).

LaRue, Jamie, and Gene Hainer. 2012. "Colorado Ebook Manifesto." *Myliblog* (July 6). <http://jaslarue.blogspot.com/2012/07/colorado-ebook-manifesto.html> (accessed November 18, 2012).

Leverkus, Cathy. 2011. "Book App Mania." *Library Media Connection* 30 (2): 50–51.

————. 2013. Personal experience.

Leverkus, Cathy, and Shannon Acedo. 2012. "eBooks." (unpublished survey).

The Library of Congress. 2011. "Finding Ebooks: a Guide." (March 18). <http://www.loc.gov/rr/program/bib/ebooks/> (accessed June 17, 2013).

————. 2012. "Libray of Congress Ebooks." (November 5). <http://www.loc.gov/rr/program/bib/ebooks/lcresources.html> (accessed June 17, 2013).

Library Journal. 2012a. *2012 Ebook Usage in U.S. Academic Libraries.* <www.thedigitalshift.com/research/ebook-usage-reports/academic> (accessed May 6, 2013).

————. 2012b. *2012 Ebook Usage in U.S. Public Libraries.* <www.thedigitalshift.com/research/ebook-usage-reports/public> (accessed May 6, 2013).

Maloney, Jennifer. 2012. "Libraries Cut E-book Deal with Penguin." *Wall Street Journal* (June 20). <http://online.wsj.com/article/SB10001424052702304898704577479174051216172.html> (accessed August 24, 2012).

"ManyBooks.net: The Best EBooks at the Best Price: Free!" n.d. <http://manybooks.net> (accessed March 26, 2013).

Marx, Anthony W. 2013. "E-Books and Democracy." *The New York Times* (May 1). <www.nytimes.com/2013/05/01/opinion/e-books-libraries-and-democracy.html?_r=0> (accessed May 25, 2012).

Microsoft. 2013. [Surface homepage]. <www.microsoft.com/Surface/en-US> (accessed March 29, 2013).

Milliot, Jim. 2013. "Macmillan to Begin E-book Library Lending Pilot." *Publishers Weekly* (January 24). <www.publishersweekly.com/pw/by-topic/digital/retailing/article/55630-macmillan-to-begin-e-book-library-lending-pilot.html> (accessed March 16, 2013).

Minow, Mary. 2013. "Copyright Licensing and the Law of E-Books. (ALA TechSource Workshop)." <www.slideshare.net/ALATechSource/ala-webinar-feb69am> (accessed March 8, 2013).

Monroe, Juli. 2013. "DOJ Approves Penguin Random House Merger—Comments." <www.teleread.com/random-house/doj-approves-penguin-random-house-merger> (accessed April 4, 2013).

Monson, Doug. 2012. Personal e-mail correspondence. 3M Cloud Library Sales Specialist. December 11.

Mueller, Joe. 2012. Personal e-mail correspondence. Vendor representative. OverDrive. January 7.

MyLibraryNYC. n.d. "About." <http://mylibrarynyc.org/about> (accessed May 5, 2013).

National Federation of the Blind. 2012. "National Federation of the Blind Applauds Settlement with Free Library of Philadelphia; Lawsuit by Four Blind Patrons over Inaccessible E-readers Resolved." <https://nfb.org/national-federation-blind-applauds-settlement-free-library-philadelphia> (accessed February 9, 2013).

National Science Foundation. n.d. "Mosaic: The Original Browser." <www.nsf.gov/about/history/nsf0050/internet/mosaic.htm> (accessed March 26, 2013).

Newman, Jared. 2012. "Ebook Publishers Want Library Borrowing to Be Difficult." *PCWorld* (February 13). <www.pcworld.com/

article/249862/e_book_publishers_want_library_borrowing_to_
be_difficult.html> (accessed April 4, 2013).

OCLC. 2013a. "Find Items in Libraries Near You." <www.worldcat.
org> (accessed March 27, 2013).

———. 2013b. "OCLC WorldCat." <www.oclc.org/worldcat.
en.html> (accessed March 27, 2013).

———. 2013c. "History of Cooperation" <www.oclc.org/about/
cooperation.en.html> (accessed April 30, 2013).

Ogg, Erica. 2013. "iPad is top selling tablet, but Android now most
common tablet OS, says IDC." *GIGAOM* (May 1). <http://
gigaom.com/2013/05/01/ipad-is-top-selling-tablet-but-
android-now-most-common-tablet-os-says-idc/> (accessed June
24, 2013).

Oliver, Daniel. 2013. Personal e-mail correspondence. Chief
Operating Officer. Light Library. March 3.

OverDrive, Inc. 2013. "School Download Library Access Agreement."
(January) <http://www.overdrive.com/files/Legal/SDL-Access-
Agreement.pdf> (accessed June 17, 2013).

Oxford University Press. 2013. *New Oxford American Dictionary*,
3rd ed. <www.oxfordreference.com/view/10.1093/
acref/9780195392883.001.0001/acref-9780195392883> (accessed
April 1, 2013).

Polanka, Sue. 2013. "Purchasing E-Books for Your Library."
<www.alatechsource.org/blog/2013/02/sue-polankas-slides-
purchasing-e-books-for-your-library.html> (accessed March 8,
2013).

Price, Gary. 2013. "Impelsys Introduces EBook Ordering System
for Libraries, Developed in Partnership with Douglas County
Libraries." *INFOdocket* (February 14). <www.infodocket.
com/2013/02/14/impelsys-introduces-ebook-ordering-system-
for-libraries-developed-in-partnership-with-douglas-county-
libraries> (accessed February 18, 2013).

Project Gutenberg. 2013. "Free Ebooks—Project Gutenberg." <www.
gutenberg.org> (accessed March 27, 2013).

"ProQuest to Acquire Ebook Library." 2013. *Publishers Weekly* (January 22). 2013. <www.publishersweekly.com/pw/by-topic/digital/content-and-e-books/article/55591-proquest-to-acquire-ebook-library.html> (accessed February 9, 2013).

Prout, JoAnn. 2013. Personal e-mail correspondence. Youth Collection Development Librarian. Omaha Public Library. January 3.

Rare Book Room. n.d. [homepage]. <www.rarebookroom.org> (accessed March 27, 2013).

Refsnes Data. 2013. "HTML Introduction." <www.w3schools.com/html/html_intro.asp> (accessed March 27, 2013).

Reid, Calvin. 2012. "Penguin Severs Ties with OverDrive." *Publisher's Weekly* (February 9). <http://www.publishersweekly.com/pw/by-topic/digital/content-and-e-books/article/50579-penguin-severs-ties-with-overdrive.html> (accessed May 30, 2013).

"Report: Penguin to Cease Windowing Library Ebook Titles." 2013. *Digital Book World* (March 27). <www.digitalbookworld.com/2013/report-penguin-to-cease-windowing-library-ebook-titles> (accessed May 12, 2013).

Roberts, Jacob. 2013. "ALA Honors Five Local Libraries for Offering Cutting-Edge Services." *District Dispatch – News for Friends of Libraries from the ALA Washington Office* (January 22). <www.districtdispatch.org/2013/01/cutting-edge-2013> (accessed April 4, 2013).

Robertson, Adi. 2013. "Macmillan Will Soon Sell Its Ebooks to Libraries for the First Time." *The Verge* (January 25). <www.theverge.com/2013/1/25/3916160/macmillan-pilot-program-will-sell-ebooks-to-libraries-for-first-time> (accessed May 11, 2013).

Russell, Carrie. 2012. "Complete Copyright for K-12 Librarians and Educators." Chicago: ALA.

Ruttig, Laura. 2013. Personal e-mail correspondence. Account Executive Educational and Library Sales OveDrive. June 19.

Sauer, Aubrey. 2013. Personal e-mail correspondence. Inside Sales. Alexandria Library Automation. March 16.

Schmidt, Colette, Mindy Null, and Kimberly Pakowski. 2011. "Nooks and EBooks: How They Look in a High School Library." (October 27). <www.ala.org/aasl/ecollab/nooks-and-ebooks> (accessed March 28, 2013).

Scholastic, Inc. 2013. "BookFlix: Program Overview." <http://teacher.scholastic.com/products/bookflixfreetrial/programoverview.htm> (accessed May 2, 2013).

School Library Journal. 2012. *2012 Ebook Usage in U.S. School (K–12) Libraries*. <www.thedigitalshift.com/research/ebook-usage-reports/k12> (accessed May 1, 2013).

Segan, Sacha. 2013. "Apple iPod touch (16GB)." *PC Magazine* (June 04). <www.pcmag.com/article2/0,2817,2419705,00.asp> (accessed June 24, 2013).

Sharp, Alex. 2010. "An iPod for Books: A Short History of Significant eBook eReaders." (March 25). <http://suite101.com/article/an-ipod-for-books-a--short-history-of-significant-ebook-ereaders-a281334> (accessed June 24, 2013).

Seymour Science LLC. 2012. "Common Core State Standards." <http://starwalk.testtexture.com/common-core.html> (accessed May 2, 2013).

Seymour Science LLC. 2013. "StarWalk Kids Media: Your Digital Media Solution. 2013." <www.starwalkkids.com/about-us/our-mission.html> (accessed May 30, 2013).

Simon & Schuster, Inc. 2013. "Archway Publishing from Simon and Schuster." <www.archwaypublishing.com> (accessed July 3, 2012).

Simpson, Carol. 2010. "Copyright for Schools: A Practical Guide." Santa Barbara, CA: ABC-Clio.

Smashwords, Inc. 2013. "About Smashwords." (December). <www.smashwords.com/about> (accessed June 5, 2013).

Snell, Sam. 2013. Personal e-mail correspondence. Customer Technical Support, Brain Hive. March 29.

Sony Electronics Inc. 2012. "Terms of Service." <https://ebookstore.sony.com/termsofservice.html> (accessed February 25, 2013).

———. 2013. "Free eBooks using 'Library Finder.'" <http://ebooks. custhelp.com/app/answers/list/kw/library%20finder/r_id/166/sno/1/search/1/session/L3RpbWUvMTM3MDQ2NDMxMi9zaWQvTk0xZnhfcmw%3D> (accessed January 2, 2013).

———. 2013. "Reader Digital Book." <http://store.sony.com/c/Sony-Reader-Digital-Books-eReader-WiFi/en/c/S_Portable_Reader> (accessed January 2, 2013).

Sparks, David. 2011. "Forget Fancy Formatting: Why Plain Text Is Best." <www.macworld.com/article/1161549/forget_fancy_formatting_why_plain_text_is_best.html> (accessed March 27, 2013).

Stone, Brad. 2009. "Amazon Erases Orwell Books from Kindle." *New York Times* (July 17). <www.nytimes.com/2009/07/18/technology/companies/18amazon.html?_r=0> (accessed May 11, 2013).

Sullivan, Maureen. 2012. "An Open Letter to America's Publishers from ALA President Maureen Sullivan." <www.ala.org/news/pr?id=11508> (accessed January 2, 2013).

———. 2013a. "ALA President, Maureen Sullivan: ALA, E-Books and You." <www.youtube.com/watch?v=8EIacd6vlvE> (accessed March 27, 2013).

———. 2013b. "Penguin Lifts Library Ebook Purchase Embargo." *The Digital Shift* (March 17). <www.thedigitalshift.com/2013/03/ebooks/penguin-lifts-library-ebook-purchase-embargo/> (accessed June 7, 2013).

Swados, Harvey. 2003. "A Revolution in Reading: 1935–1960." <www.crcstudio.org/paperbacks> (accessed May 12, 2013).

Tech Media Network. 2013. "2013 Best eBook Reader Reviews and Comparisons." <http://ebook-reader-review.toptenreviews.com> (accessed June 5, 2013).

Thomas, Lisa C. 2011. "New Technologies, New Directions Emerge at ALA 2011." *American Libraries* (July 13). <http://americanlibrariesmagazine.org/features/07132011/new-technologies-new-directions-emerge-ala-2011> (accessed December 31, 2012).

3M. 2006. *3M Standard Interchange Protocol*, Rev. 2.12. <http://
multimedia.3m.com/mws/mediawebserver?6666660Zjcf6lVs6EV
s66S0LeCOrrrrQ-> (accessed March 29, 2013).

————. 2013. "3M™ Cloud eReaders & Discovery Stations." <http://
solutions.3m.com/wps/portal/3M/en_US/library-systems-
NA/library-technologies/ebook-lending/Cloud-eReaders/>
(accessed July 1, 2013).

Tobin, Julie. 2012. Conversation District Account Manager. Baker &
Taylor School Libraries. June 19.

Toor, Amar. 2011. "3M Announces Cloud Library E-book Lending
Service for '21st Century' Libraries." <www.engadget.
com/2011/05/20/3m-announces-cloud-library-e-book-lending-
service-for-21st-cent> (accessed March 29, 2013).

TumbleBookLibrary. n.d. [homepage] <www.tumblebooks.com>
(accessed November 23, 2012).

"UPDATED: Macmillan Announces Details of Library Lending
Pilot." 2013. *INFOdocket* (January 24). <www.infodocket.
com/2013/01/24/macmillan-announces-details-of-library-
lending-pilot> (accessed January 24, 2013).

U.S. Copyright Office. 2012. "Copyright: Fair Use." <www.copyright.
gov/fls/fl102.html> (accessed March 09, 2013).

U.S. Department of Education, Office for Civil Rights. 2011. "FAQ."
<www2.ed.gov/about/offices/list/ocr/docs/dcl-ebook-faq-
201105.html> (accessed February 9, 2013).

Vidal, Marcia. 2013. Conversation. Vendor representative. Gale
Ciengage Learning. February 7.

Vinjamuri, David. 2013. "Simon & Schuster Tests EBook Lending
With New York Libraries." *Forbes.* (April 15). <http://www.
forbes.com/sites/davidvinjamuri/2013/04/15/simon-schuster-
tests-ebook-lending-with-new-york-libraries/> (accessed June 28,
2013).

Wikimedia Foundation. 2013a. "Comparison of E-book Formats."
Wikipedia. <http://en.wikipedia.org/wiki/Comparison_of_e-
book_formats> (accessed June 4, 2013).

———. 2013b. "Copyright Act of 1976." *Wikipedia.* <http://en.wikipedia.org/wiki/Copyright_Act_of_1976> (accessed June 15, 2013).

———. 2013c. "Windows 8." *Wikipedia.* <http://en.wikipedia.org/wiki/Windows_8> (accessed March 27, 2013).

Worchester Polytechnic Institute. 2010. "Overview of the Digital Millennium Copyright Act (DMCA)." <www.wpi.edu/offices/policies/copyright/dmca.html> (accessed February 19, 2013).

World Digital Library. n.d. "Mission." <www.wdl.org/en/about> (accessed April 19, 2013).

Zickuhr, Kathryn, et. al. 2013. "Younger Americans' Library Habits and Expectations". *Pew Internet* (June 25). < http://libraries.pewinternet.org/2013/06/25/younger-americans-library-services/> (accessed June 26, 2013).

Zimmermann, Kim. 2012. "Reference: Computer History." <http://www.livescience.com/20718-computer-history.html> (accessed April 16, 2013).

Resources

Archived Presentations and Conferences

Sometimes presentations that were part of e-events are archived online. The resources below will be of interest to school librarians exploring ideas related to use of ebooks in schools.

"Copyright, Licensing, and the Law of E-Books" by Mary Minow
<www.slideshare.net/ALATechSource/ala-webinar-feb69am>

"No Shelf Required 2: Use and Management of Electronic Books"
by Sue Polanka <www.alatechsource.org/blog/2013/02/sue-polankas-slides-purchasing-e-books-for-your-library.html>

"Choosing an eBook Platform(s) for Your K12 School Library" by
Buffy Hamilton <www.slideshare.net/buffyjhamilton/choosing-an-ebook-platform-that-works-for-your-k12-library-13917868>

"Libraries, Ebooks and Beyond" <http://www.thedigitalshift.com/events/ebooks-and-beyond>

Blogs

The authors of the blogs on this list often address issues relating to providing e-resources to students, or review hardware and software related to ebook useage.

The Digital Shift: Library Journal, School Library Journal on Libraries and New Media <www.thedigitalshift.com>

eBookAnoid: Reviewing eReaders, eBooks, eBook websites and All Things Related to eBooks and eReaders <http://ebookanoid.com>

Electronic Frontier Foundation: Defending Your Rights in the Digital World <www.eff.org>

Evoke: Creating the Future for Library E-content <http://evoke.cvlsites. org>

INFOdocket <www.infodocket.com> by Gary Price for *Library Journal*

Myliblog <http://jaslarue.blogspot.com> by James LaRue

No Shelf Required <www.libraries.wright.edu/noshelfrequired> moderated by Sue Polanka

Pew Internet <www.pewinternet.org>

PWxyz: The News Blog of Publishers Weekly <http://blogs. publishersweekly.com/blogs/PWxyz>

Scoop.it! Shine on the Web <www.scoop.it>

TeleRead: News & Views on E-Books, Libraries, Publishing and Related Topics <www.teleread.com>

21st Century Library Blog <http://21stcenturylibrary.com> by Steve Matthews

21st Century Libraries [on Scoop.it]: All Things 21st Century Library Related <www.scoop.it/t/21st-century-libraries> curated by Steve Matthews

The Unquiet Librarian <http://theunquietlibrarian.wordpress.com> by Buffy Hamilton

ZDNet <www.zdnet.com>

Ebook Publishers and Vendors

Free Ebook Collections

Feedbooks <www.feedbooks.com>
International Children's Digital Library
    <http://en.childrenslibrary.org>
Kobo <www.kobobooks.com>
The Library of Congress <http://archive.org/details/library_of_
    congress>
ManyBooks.net <http://manybooks.net>
Rare Book Room <http://rarebookroom.org>

Large Free Ebook Collections

Digital Public Library of America (DPLA) <http://dp.la>
Google Books <http://books.google.com>
HathiTrust <www.hathitrust.org>
Open Library <http://openlibrary.org>
Project Gutenberg <www.gutenberg.org>
World Digital Library <www.wdl.org/en>

Elementary and Middle School Vendors

BookFlix <http://teacher.scholastic.com/products/bookflixfreetrial/
    index.htm>
StarWalk Kids Media <www.starwalkkids.com/about-us/our-
    mission.html>

K–12+ Vendors

Baker & Taylor (B&T) Axis 360 platform <http://btol.com/axis360>
Brain Hive <www.brainhive.com/Pages/Home.aspx>
Capstone Digital <www.capstonepub.com/content/DIGITAL_CIL>
FollettShelf <www.aboutfollettebooks.com/follettshelf.cfm>
OverDrive <www.overdrive.com>
Smashwords <www.smashwords.com>

3M Cloud Library <http://3m-ssd.implex.net/cloudapps/index.html>

TumbleBookLibrary and **TumbleBookCloud** <www.tumblebooks.com>

Content Management Platforms

EBSCO Discovery Service <www.ebscohost.com/discovery>
MackinVIA <www.mackin.com/eServices/MACKIN-VIA.aspx>

Nonfiction Collection

American Council Of Learned Sociaties- Humanities E-Book (ACLS-HEB) <http://humanitiesebook.org/about-us/default.html>
Credo <http://corp.credoreference.com/index.php>
EBSCOhost ebook collections <www.ebscohost.com/ebooks>
Gale Virtual Reference Library Platform (GVRL) <www.gale.cengage.com/servlet/GvrlMS?msg=ma>
Ingram MyiLibrary <www.myilibrary.com>
JSTOR <http://books.jstor.org>
ProQuest ebrary <www.proquest.com/en-US/products/brands/pl_ebrary.shtml>

Additional Sources of Nonficton

ABC-CLIO <http://ebooks.abc-clio.com/main.aspx>
Infobase <www.infobasepublishing.com>
Oxford <www.oxford-ebooks.com/oe2/index.php>
Rosen <www.rosenpublishing.com>
Salem Press <http://salempress.com/store/pages/ebooks.htm>
Scholastic <http://store.scholastic.com/landing-page/landingpage/storia/shop-ebooks>

Webinars

Webinars of interest to school librarians who want to learn about ways to incorporate e-resources in their library collections and programs are available from a number of sources, including those listed below.

LearningTimes's Handheld Librarian Online Conference <http://handheldlibrarian.org>

ALA TechSource <www.alatechsource.org>

AASL eCOLLAB <www.ala.org/aasl/ecollab>

School Library Journal webcasts <www.slj.com/category/webcasts>

ABC-CLIO <www.abc-clio.com>

Follett <www.follettsoftware.com/webinars.cfm>

Library Media Connection <www.librarymediaconnection.com>

Publications from AASL

American Association of School Librarians offers a rich variety of publications on topics essential to school librarians everywhere. To read descriptions of each publication and to order, go to <www.ala.org/aasl/booksproducts>. Order online at <www.alastore.ala.org/aasl>.

Learning Standards & Program Guidelines

Standards for the 21st-Century Learner (2007)
> Available for free download (PDF) at <www.ala.org/aasl/standards>. Packets of full-color brochures may also be purchased.

Standards for the 21st-Century Learner in Action (2009)

Empowering Learners: Guidelines for School Library Programs (2009)

A Planning Guide for Empowering Learners with School Library Program Assessment Rubric (2010)
> Available for purchase at <www.aasl.eb.com>, or for more information and resources visit <www.ala.org/aasl/planningguide>.

A 21st-Century Approach to School Librarian Evaluation (2012) **NEW!**

Library Spaces for 21st-Century Learners: A Planning Guide for Creating New School Library Concepts (2013) **NEW!**

Empowering Leadership: Developing Behaviors for Success (2013) **NEW!**

Other AASL Publications

Assessing Student Learning in the School Library Media Center (2007)

Best of *Knowledge Quest* series:

Instructional Partnerships: A Pathway to Leadership (2013) **NEW!**

School Library Media Programs in Action: Civic Engagement, Social Justice, and Equity (2009)

School Library Services in a Multicultural Society (2009)

Collection Development for the School Library Media Program (2006)

Every Student Reads: Collaboration and Reading to Learn (2005)

The Power of Data: An Introduction to Using Local, State, and National Data to Support School Library Programs (2012) **NEW!**

Advocacy Tools

School Library Programs Create Lifelong Learners: A Student's and Parent's Guide to Evaluating Independent School Libraries (2011)

Advocacy Brochure Series: *School Library Programs Improve Student Learning* (2011)

Available for free download (PDF) at <www.ala.org/aasl/ advocacybrochures>. Packets of full-color brochures may also be purchased.

AASL Position Statement on Digital Content and E-books in School Library Collections

Today's twenty-first century students must be able to discover, analyze, evaluate, interpret, and communicate ideas, information and knowledge in a variety of ways. Because school library programs are instrumental in teaching these skills, their collections must include a wide variety of formats beyond printed books. These multiple formats, including e-books and other forms of digital content, should be accessible by the school community physically and virtually as indicated in the mission statement of AASL's program guidelines, *Empowering Learners: Guidelines for School Library Programs* (AASL 2009). School library programs should provide access to materials in all formats, provide students and staff with current resources, and anticipate changes in technology.

Presently, in 2013, there is no single device that will access all e-books. Consequently, school librarians face a confusing investment decision. Some e-books are included in subscription databases, others are available in lease-only contracts, and still others are available for direct purchase for the life of the school's need for the title. Contributing to the confusion, some e-books may be read only by one person at a time while other titles can be purchased for simultaneous access by multiple readers. Many free e-books may be read on a variety of devices; however, the number of free quality titles is limited.

In this age of instant access to information and because the AASL school library program mission statement is to "ensure that students and staff are effective users of ideas and information," schools should begin to provide anytime/anywhere access to reliable digital content. This mission is accomplished by:

- Updating selection policies to encompass digital content and reader devices;

- Determining the best allocation of funding for digital content and reader devices by knowing the school community, recognizing early adopters and followers, and listening to all learning needs;

- Ensuring that access to portable electronic devices and digital content is available to all students, no matter their off-campus situations;

- Ensuring there are no financial barriers to electronic devices or resources;

- Buying portable electronic devices that will support the widest variety of e-book formats;

- Considering the age of the learners in selecting e-readers and/ or other digital devices, remembering both hand sizes and content needs.

- Recognizing that vendors may package groups of titles, subscription databases and/or e-book collections, together, perhaps including some titles less useful to the specific school curriculum, resulting in the need to purchase overlapping products;

- Recognizing that not all titles are yet available digitally and that schools still need to have printed books available;

- Selecting materials for the variety of challenged learners, offering auditory and visually supportive formats;

- Acknowledging that today's digital reading devices may be outdated within two years and that funding will be needed to continually update devices and content formats;
- Accepting the use of student-owned devices on school networks;
- Guaranteeing the right to privacy when and if vendors collect data on what students read;
- Cataloging all digital content while developing ways to publicize the availability of these resources because budget expenditures are only justified when students and faculty are aware of the resources and actively use them;
- Developing and participating in cooperative purchasing agreements and consortia as a way to ease costs and share ownership;
- Exploring new business models for purchasing resources, including the use of credit cards noting that digital resources are not so easily purchased using traditional purchase order procedures.

Digital content, e-books, e-readers and other digital devices are essential components of school library collections. These collections will remain in a period of transition for some time while school librarians balance the selection of devices and formats, including print, e-book and digital materials. Schools and districts will need to provide funding and support for this powerful means to access information, and for the requisite experimentation in the face of ever-changing options. Librarians and administrators need a cooperative spirit of tolerance as we explore emerging digital devices and new ways of purchasing and lending materials. It is an exciting time as we move ever forward into the twenty-first century.

Brief Definitions
- Digital content is any content that is published in digital form. This includes online encyclopedias and subscription databases that contain keyword-searchable articles and/or

e-books. Digital content is accessed live via the Internet and subscription databases; it may be leased or purchased directly from vendors. Such content may be downloaded.

- E-books are books read on digital devices including hand-held electronic devices and even computers; they may contain hyperlinks to other resources. E-books may be purchased, downloaded free from public domain or Creative Commons, or "borrowed" through library subscription services.

- E-book readers are portable electronic devices that can be used to read digital books or periodicals. With Internet access and storage for downloaded content, they are designed to operate for long hours using minimal power. Some proprietary devices have access only to e-books from the same vendor. Other hardware devices, both mobile (smartphones, PDAs, pocket and tablet PCs) and desktop, are loosely defined as E-book readers because they can read e-books. These devices can do more than access e-books, but are not designed specifically for reading books for long hours using minimal power.

- Audiobooks are spoken texts, often available as digital downloads. While not considered e-books, audiobooks are sometimes included in the definition of digital content.

Adopted 06/28/13
Source: www.ala.org/aasl/advocacy/resources/position-statements

D

Glossary

aggregator — Aggregator-managed circulation and access are based on the federated-search model. Any databases, ebooks, and other digital resources that the library leases or subscribes to can be searched from one platform provided by the aggregator.

AZW formatting language — AZW is the original formatting language for ebooks sold by Amazon; ebooks in this format can be read only on the Kindle family of readers.

book apps — Book apps are electronic books developed by authors, illustrators, software architects and digital artists; the books work with touch technology that allows readers to interact with the illustrations and text.

bundler — A bundler is a vendor who sells bundles of ebooks instead of individual titles. Typically, the resources in the bundle were selected by the vendor for inclusion, not by the customer.

database/ebook interface — Ebooks and databases are similar in that both are collections of information organized in a particular way. Some publishers (such as Salem Press) present both ebook and database forms of their titles; their distinction is that the database cannot be downloaded, cannot be accessed on all e-readers, and can no longer be accessed when a new edition of the title is available.

developer — A developer is a company that selects authors, illustrators, software architects, and digital artists, and then the team organizes, edits, publishes, and advertises a book app or interactive ebook.

devices — In the context of ebooks, devices are the hardware for reading ebooks; these devices include smartphones, MP3 touch players (such as the iPod), dedicated e-readers, tablets, laptops, and desktop computers.

Digital Millennium Copyright Act (DMCA) — The DMCA is legislation passed in 1998 as an addition to the existing copyright laws, which had been passed before e-resources were widely used; DMCA governs use of online and electronic resources.

DPLA, Digital Public Library of America (dp.la) — DPLA is an open, freely distributed network of digital materials collected from many libraries, universities, and museums nationwide, including the Smithsonian Institute, Harvard University, and New York Public Library.

digital rights management (DRM) — DRM refers to restrictions placed on electronic books by the publisher or author that control the use the book (e.g., how long the ebook can be circulated by the library before the ebook must be purchased again and whether that book can be leant or given to another user); DRM enforcement usually involves codes and small software programs built into ebook files.

embargo — In the context of ebooks, an embargo is the delay between when an item is published in hardcopy and when it is available for distribution through databases or other platforms. Intended to protect the market for hardcopy books, especially best sellers, embargos are usually structured by book and journal publishers to maintain exclusivity for a specified period of time.

ePub formatting language — ePub files are produced using an open-standard formatting language that most e-readers can read; this open-standard language can be used by any publisher or individual; it is not proprietary.

e-reader apps—E-reader apps, created by e-reader distributors such as Amazon and OverDrive, allow ebooks to be downloaded to individual e-reader devices and managed, either offline or in the cloud.

Fair Use—Fair Use is a category of legal allowances granting limited use of copyrighted materials by those in areas such as teaching, news reporting, and literary criticism.

formatting language—In the context of ebooks, formatting language is software language used to create files that support use of hypertext, hyperlinks, touch technology, and other tools that might be used to create ebooks.

friction—In the context of ebooks, friction is delay that may be built into ebook management systems to slow down access to ebooks through public libraries; if friction is high, patrons may decide to buy the ebook instead of borrowing from the library.

HTML—Hypertext Markup Language is a formatting language in which tags indicate the configuration, design, and display of the page; websites are usually written in HTML.

HTML tags—HTML tags are programming prompts that direct the design and display of text read with a browser application and can hyperlink webpages to each other (e.g., <HTML> <Head>, <Body>).

hyperlink—A hyperlink is a text string that, when clicked or tapped, opens another page, a graphic, or other element that supplements the text.

hypertext—Hypertext is a collection of digital resources linked using HTML tags; hypertext can also refer to the text string in a hyperlink.

iBook app—An iBook app is an e-reader app used to read ebooks purchased from the iBookstore, which provides access to books in Apple's customized ePub format.

iBook formatting language—The iBook formatting language is a proprietary formatting language based on the ePub standard; this proprietary language was developed by Apple for creating ebooks using iBook Author.

integrated library system (ILS) — An ILS is a library management system that administers the circulation, cataloging, and patron access for all the resources owned by a library.

iOS — iOS, originally "iPhone O(perating) S(ystem)", is the operating system (underlying software on which apps run) for mobile devices; originally developed by Apple for iPhones and iPods, iOS is now used on a wide variety of Apple products; iOS is not licensed to nonproprietary devices.

license agreements/EULA ("End-User Licensing Agreement") — A licensing agreement states the terms and conditions under which software or a digital resource can be used. In the context of ebooks, the EULA is the (often extensive) "fine print" to which users must agree before downloading or using proprietary e-resources.

MOBI formatting language — MOBI files are formatted with HTML tags to create ebook pages designed for mobile devices; though they can be read on most e-readers and mobile devices, images in MOBI files sometimes don't display well on devices with larger screens.

MP3/iPod touch — An iPod or other MP3 player with a touch screen can be used to read or listen to ebooks; MP3 players typically can display ebooks only in plain text or rich text format.

multiuser access — A license for multiuser access allows more than one user to simultaneously access the same e-resource; the number of simultaneous users is specified in the licensing agreement.

open source formatting language — Open source languages are not proprietary; in the context of ebooks, open source languages are developed for all e-readers that do not require a proprietary format and are available to the general public for publishing ebooks.

patron-driven acquisition (PDA) — PDA is an acquisition model used by some vendors who post all available titles in the collection, including those for which the library does not have access; when one particular title is requested multiple times by the faculty or students the library has the option of purchasing that title.

plain text formatting — Plain text (a.k.a. ASCII text) does not contain hyperlinks, tags, or formatting commands and can be read without a reader app on any machine with any operating system.

platform—In the context of ebooks, a platform is a website designed to display ebooks from a specific vendor or publisher; some ebooks can be read directly from the platform, while others require use of an e-reader app.

proprietary formatting language—A proprietary formatting language is any language that has been developed to be used by a single company's e-reader family or by one ebook publishing tool. A proprietary language is rarely available for use by entities outside the company that owns the language.

publisher—A publisher is a company that selects authors and illustrators, organizes, edits, disseminates, and advertises books and/or ebooks.

publisher disclaimers—Publisher disclaimers are often found in the End-User License Agreement (EULA) and include the terms under which the publisher will license the product; sample disclaimers in license agreements for ebooks include such language as "for the individual, non-commercial, revocable, non-transferrable use of the licensee."

purchase-on-demand (POD)—POD is the model in which libraries purchase ebooks (and other items) as they are requested by students or faculty.

Right of First Sale/First Sale Doctrine—Right of First Sale refers to the rights granted to purchasers of copyrighted material, recognized by the U.]S. Supreme Court in 1908 and codified in 1976, including the right to sell, give away, or otherwise dispose of a particular copy of a book, record, CD, movie, etc.

self-publishing—Self-publishing is the process by which writers manage the production and distribution of their books by themselves, without the formal involvement of a commercial publisher. This process can be done with the assistance of several types of self-publishing software.

touch technology—Touch technology is used to create computer screens that respond to physical input (tapping or swiping) from a stylus or finger.

unlimited simultaneous access—Unlimited simultaneous access allows an unlimited number of users to access a licensed e-resource simultaneously.

vendor — In the context of ebooks, a vendor designs (or buys) platforms and e-reading applications to deliver ebooks from various publishers to their customers'; the services are provided through licensing agreements or subscriptions.

Index

American Council of Learned
Societies–Humanities E-book
(ACLS-HEB), 24-25, 29, 66, 120, 122,
196
American Library Association (ALA),
15, 75, 91, 95, 105, 135, 145, 156
Americans with Disabilities Act
(ADA), 148, 149
Android. *See* Operating system
Apple. *See* Ebook vendors and
publishers
Apple iBook. *See* iBook
Apple iPad. *See* iPad
Apple iTunes. *See* iTunes
Archival Preservation. *See* Copying
digital works
Archway Publishing, 46
Association of Canadian Publishers,
170
Audiobooks and audio digital books,
17-22 40, 204
Authors for Library Ebooks, 12, 15
Axis 360. *See* Baker & Taylor
AZW formatting language. *See*
Formatting language

B

Baker & Taylor. *See* Ebook vendors
and publishers
      Axis 360, 9, 19, 20-21,114, 116,
        117, 118
Barnes & Noble. *See* Ebook vendors
and publishers
Bay Area Independent School
Librarians (BAISL), 137, 138
Bay Area Library and Information
System, 116
Behler, Ann, 86, 95, 144
BiblioTech, Bexar County Texas, 171
Big Six publishers, 15, 16, 98, 116, 133,
157, 158
Blio e-reader app. *See* E-reader apps
Blogs, 96, 103-104, 194
Bluefire Reader app. *See* E-reader apps
Book apps, 3, 5, 17, 205
BookExpo America, 160

Bookflix. *See* Ebook vendors and
publishers
Brain Hive. See Ebook vendors and
publishers
Brantley, Peter, 115, 170-171
Brentwood School, East Campus,
73-74, 93-94
Bring Your Own Device (BYOD)
programs, 52, 68-70, 86,140
Britannica Publishing. *See* Ebook
vendors and publishers
Browsability, 3, 162, 164
Budget, 86, 95, 101, 106, 131-133
Bundle, purchase, 28-29, 41, 78, 102,
113, 138, 171, 205
Bundler , 110, 112, 113, 205

C

Califa Library Group, 12, 116
Call numbers in cataloging, 123
Capital Records, LLC v. ReDigi Inc. See
First sale and Redigi lawsuit
Capstone Digital. *See* Ebook vendors
and publishers
Capstone myOn, 18, 35, 141
Cataloging, 121+
Cataloging loaded devices, 124-125
Cherry Creek School District (Denver,
Co), 142
Choosing vendors. *See* Vendors,
choosing
Circulating ebooks, legality. *See*
Legality of circulating ebook
devices
Circulating e-readers. *See* E-readers
Circulating loaded devices, 14, 79, 150,
149, 179
Circulation
    limits, 4, 97
    policies for devices, 69, 81,
        150
    policies for ebooks, 80-81, 96,
        100, 114
    public libraries, 1-2, 168, 170
    school libraries, 2
Collection analysis, 95-96

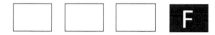

Tables & Figures

Tables

Figures